Ruby for Beginners:
Your Guide To Easily Learn Ruby Programming in 7 Days

By iCode Academy

D1409961

Table of Contents

INTRODUCTION: 5

CHAPTER 1: GETTING ACQUAINTED WITH RUBY   8

WHAT IS RUBY PROGRAMMING   8
BRIEF HISTORY OF RUBY   13
CODES, EVALUATION, OBJECTS, METHODS, CLASSES, AND INSTANCES   17

CHAPTER 2: INITIAL PREPARATIONS   22

RUBY INSTALLATION   22
DOCUMENTATION, CLASSES, METHODS, AND MORE   27

CHAPTER 3: START WITH THE BASICS   30

GETTING FAMILIAR WITH STRINGS, SYMBOLS, NUMBERS, AND NIL   30
RUBY OPERATIONS   34
TYPE CONVERSION AND OTHERS   39

CHAPTER 4: RUBY VARIABLES   44

UNDERSTANDING VARIABLES   44
USER INPUT AND VARIABLE SCOPE   51
TYPES OF VARIABLES   55

CHAPTER 5: ALL ABOUT METHODS   57

WHAT ARE METHODS?   57
MUTATING THE CALLER AND MORE ON PUTS AND RETURN   61
CHAINING METHODS AND ARGUMENTS   66

CHAPTER 6: FLOW CONTROL   71

CONDITIONALS   71
COMBINING EXPRESSIONS   79
CASE STATEMENT   83

CHAPTER 7: ITERATORS AND LOOPS 86

SIMPLE LOOP 86
THE DIFFERENT LOOPS 92
CONDITIONALS, ITERATORS, AND RECURSION 101

CHAPTER 8: MORE ON ARRAYS AND HASHES 107

ARRAYS 107
ARRAY METHODS AND HASHES 112
MORE ON HASHES 118

CONCLUSION: 122

OTHER BOOKS BY ICODE ACADEMY 123

DID YOU ENJOY THIS BOOK? 124

INTRODUCTION:

Welcome to this training for the Kindle...

This book aims to guide a complete novice in Ruby programming. This book is carefully crafted to aid the new or inexperienced programmer in learning to write a code in Ruby language. If you are someone who somehow developed a fear to explore the unknown and still interested to learn Ruby programming, then this book can truly help you.

This book covers everything that a beginner in Ruby programming should learn. Understand that programming offers an infinite amount of information and knowledge. However, this book understands that it may overwhelm a mere beginner in programming if it tackles even the advanced features of the Ruby language.

This book can help you build a solid, basic knowledge in programming that can help you a lot when you begin to write your own program in Ruby language. You can use the acquired knowledge to pursue or learn more about Ruby's advanced concepts later on. For now, just concentrate on the basics and make sure to absorb every lesson before you go to the next one.

Practice makes perfect and this book provides a lot of practice programs or exercises that can help you enhance your experience in Ruby programming. The exercises are simple and easy to understand to help you comprehend the lesson quickly. You also need to take note of the error messages that you may encounter. Let them serve as your guide so you can avoid the same mistake in the future or help you resolve the same error when you encounter them once more.

Coding a program is often perceived as something difficult to accomplish. To be blunt, it is not as difficult as many people think. However, it does require patience and an open mind. You sometimes need to think outside the box to find the solution that you seek, and there are several solutions to a certain problem.

You may consider yourself lucky to be able to write a short program in a jiffy. There are also cases where you may only find satisfaction when you write a long code. One thing is for certain – writing a program is never boring.

Learning Ruby programming in 7 days is not something impossible to accomplish. Even a person with a little or no experience with any programming language can learn it within those days. As you go through each lesson, you will notice that it is quite easy to understand. It becomes much simpler when you have patience and discipline.

If you made a mistake, you will see an error message on your screen. It can guide you in correcting the mistake you made in writing your code. There are lots of cases where simple capitalization or indentation is the culprit. Don't panic in case you encountered an error, let the error message guide you in correcting your codes and make your program flow according to your design.

Understand that you will be able to learn the Ruby basics in 7 days, but that won't make you an instant expert. You still need to practice and work your way in discovering the cool things that you can do with Ruby as you go along. Even expert programmers need to spend ample time in honing their programming skills. Before you know it, you are ready to create a more complex program.

This book presents everything that a novice may need in understanding the basic Ruby programming. It is presented in such a way that anyone without prior programming knowledge will find it easy to understand – most technical jargons were kept to minimal, and they are the terminologies that you will likely encounter once you have started writing your program.

You will be able to understand and recognize the terms without encountering difficulties as well as the way to do it properly. There are lots of program samples in this book together with the explanations so you will be guided properly and have fun as you learn.

If you are a fresh entrepreneur, looking for a way to earn extra income, or someone who just wants to learn new things, then this book is for you. You won't feel alienated with the terms used, and you will be able to grasp the things that the different codes try to accomplish. It is simple enough to understand, and it is rich with tips that could get you going.

The content of this book is only limited to the important, basic things that a novice programmer should know. It discusses the topics that are truly beneficial to the beginner. You can always find the advanced books on Ruby programming when you have decided to learn more to hone your skill.

You will be pleased that you picked this book to learn Ruby. See everything unfold before your eyes and learn the many things that Ruby programming can bring. You may even discover a more fulfilling career.

CHAPTER 1: GETTING ACQUAINTED WITH RUBY

WHAT IS RUBY PROGRAMMING?

Brief Description and Important Features

Benefits and Advantages of Ruby Language

Prerequisites in Learning Ruby Programming

Brief Description and Important Features

Ruby is a powerful, object-oriented programming language that Yukihiro Matsumoto developed in 1995. A programming language is said to be object-oriented if it allows the programmer to define the data type of a data structure as well as the functions or operations that can be used on the data structure.

The unmatched exquisiteness of Ruby can be found in the harmonious relationship between its power and simplicity. It has a syntax that is easy on the eye, simple to write, and natural to read. A complete beginner in programming won't feel alienated when dealing with Ruby programming language.

Ruby is a flexible programming language that can be used to create games, to process text, and/or for web development. Ruby has the following important features that you need to keep in mind:

- It is a high level language, which makes it easy to write and understand – it is similar to writing the English language. Like the usual spoken language, you need to follow the correct grammar (syntax) in writing the codes so that your machine won't have difficulty executing the commands.

- As stated earlier, it is an object-oriented language. Later, you will learn more about objects. For now, it is enough for you to know that Ruby treats everything as an object.

8

- It is an interpreted language. You don't need to use a compiler to execute or run the codes (program) in Ruby. If you have time to trace back some of the early programming languages, you will see that most of them use compilers and/or linkers to run or execute the program.

- It is easy to use because it follows the natural flow of English language. It is especially designed to cater to the human needs rather than that of a computer, which is the top reason why Ruby is easy to learn.

When you take time to trace back the early generations of the programming languages, you can just imagine the difficulties that the programmers needed to endure or overcome during such years. There was a need to think like a computer in order to write a code that would be easy for the machine to execute or run.

Benefits and Advantages of Ruby Language

There are numerous programming languages that novice and seasoned programmers can choose from. If you have decided to become a programmer now, it is advisable to choose the right language that would be able to motivate you to get going. Ruby language is easy to learn and it bears some similarities with other popular programming languages today. It would be easy for you to learn another language when you start with Ruby programming language or other similar language.

One of the objectives of Ruby is to help the web developers to create web applications in the least possible time. Another good thing about Ruby is that it's free to use. You can go to this site to download your free Ruby:

https://www.ruby-lang.org/en/

If you want to try Ruby right away, you can click this link to try the Ruby online version.

A programmer can modify the Ruby language. It makes it easy for a programmer to make the necessary changes and write the program without restrictions.

9

It also has a mark-and-sweep garbage collection that gives a programmer the ability to write the program without worrying about maintaining the reference counts in extension libraries. Ruby can also load extension libraries if your operating system permits it.

Ruby is considered a general purpose language. No one can deny its popularity. It is commonly used in Ruby on Rails applications. Companies like Kickstarter, Goodreads, Twitter, and Soundcloud chose Ruby to help them launch their products in the net.

Ruby on Rails is one of the world's best programming frameworks. There are many companies that rely on Rails. It is basically a group of shortcuts that were coded in Ruby to help you build web applications or websites within short amount of time. If you are looking for a framework that is fast and reliable, then Rails can cater to your demand and you need to learn Ruby programming for that.

Ruby is efficient and fast, which makes it one of the most worthy languages today. In this modern time, where speed and efficiency must go hand in hand, Ruby can bring a lot of advantages and benefits to businesses worldwide. Business owners know that the only way to stay alive in the competitive business arena is to give their clients efficient service without making them wait.

Ruby is easy to access and manipulate, which makes it user friendly. Its simplicity offers a lot of comfort to the user. In fact, being simple is one of Ruby's best features.

Ruby's syntax is easy to understand and follow. If you have researched about the early programming languages, then you must have noticed that the written codes sounded just like a machine. The programmer must think like a machine in order to code a program that the computer would understand. Ruby and the majority of modern programming languages use natural English language. That being said, Ruby won't put the programmer in a tricky situation.

Ruby is recognized all over the world and it has large community that you can depend on. The community continues to grow and the best Ruby programmers are part of it. As a novice programmer, you need all the help that you can get in order to develop or polish your Ruby programming skill. You can ask the community for assistance and some tips on how you can improve your ability. The Ruby community is friendly, especially with beginners.

There are available Ruby learning resources online that you can access in case you need additional info or would like to take a glimpse on the advanced courses. However, it is advisable to learn and get a good grip of the basics first.

Ruby can open a path for numerous job and/or extra income opportunities. If you are looking for a new career or would like to gain extra source of income, then being a Ruby programmer is one of the options that you may want to consider. Ruby continues to gain popularity and it is still highly in demand. Adding a skill in Ruby programming can add some spark to your resume and make potential employers or clients take interests on you.

Prerequisites in Learning Ruby Programming

You can start learning the Ruby language even if you don't have prior knowledge in programming. You may even hear some advice from experts to start learning Ruby first before trying your hands on other programming languages. However, it is recommended that you have basic knowledge on how to operate a computer and access the net.

It also helps a lot if you are familiar with the computer jargons. There are computer terminologies that are quite difficult to understand or explain. The best way to avoid nuisance while learning Ruby is to get familiar with the usual computer terminologies that are being used today. If you are already familiar with them, then you can proceed without delay.

There is no prerequisite, but there is a post-requisite framework called Ruby on Rails. You need Rails to develop mobile app, web applications, or enhance your business website. You can also use Ruby programming for the framework called Sinatra.

Between Ruby on Rails and Sinatra, most would prefer the former because it covers more of the common things that you want to do. Sinatra is small and light. It does not offer as much functionality and features of Ruby on Rails. On the other hand, Ruby on Rails must be updated quite often and must be frequently maintained. Sinatra does not need frequent update, although it still needs to get updated to function well. It is designed to be simple and slim.

There are people that prefer Sinatra over Rails because of its simplicity and low maintenance requirements.

Ruby is no doubt one of the most popular programming languages in the world. One of the main advantages of Ruby is that many programming platforms support it and it is recognized worldwide.

BRIEF HISTORY OF RUBY

The Ruby Language and its Creator

The Reasons Behind

The Start of Worldwide Recognition

The Ruby Language and its Creator

Yukihiro Matsumoto, also known as "Matz", created the Ruby programming language. He wanted a programming language that prioritizes the human needs and not those of a computer.

In 1993, Yukihiro Matsumoto and a colleague were discussing the likelihood of developing an object-oriented scripting-language. Mr. Matsumoto confirmed that he was familiar with Perl, but did not appreciate it. For him, Perl could be considered as a "toy" programming language. He also stated that he knew Python programming, but his appreciation on the said language was almost on the same level as Perl's.

The Reasons Behind

That meeting with a colleague paved way to the conception of Ruby programming language. The perfect language for Mr. Matsumoto must be a true object-oriented programming language. It should follow a simple syntax and must be user-friendly. The language must have garbage collection and exception handling. It must have closures and iterators. The programming language must be portable.

After spending time searching for the existence of such language, with no luck, Yukihiro Matsumoto finally realized that he must create his own programming language. It should have all the features that he would like to see in a perfect object-oriented programming language.

He spent several months writing an interpreter before he finally released the first public version of Ruby 0.95 in 1995. It was distributed to different Japanese domestic newsgroups. The first version of Ruby can still be downloaded today, although you may be taking a great risk doing so.

The version 1.0 of Ruby was released in December, 1996. After 8 months, Ruby 1.1 was introduced. Ruby 1.2 was the first stable version of the programming language that Matz has created. It was released in December, 1998. During such time, Ruby only circulated in Japan.

The Start of Worldwide Recognition

In 1998, a simple Ruby homepage was created and the content was written in English. At that time, Ruby was still localized. Ruby-Talk, the first Ruby mailing list in English language, was created. The purpose of its creation was to introduce Ruby to the rest of the world, and it was a complete success.

The first book on the Ruby programming language was written in October, 1999. The authors of the book, The Object-Oriented Scripting Language Ruby, were Keiju Ishitsuka and Yukihiro Matsumoto. Soon, the Ruby programming language also spread to English-speaking countries.

In 2001, Ruby's first English book called "Programming Ruby" was published. Many people got a chance to learn the language, and all thanks to the introduction of the book.

In 2003, Ruby 1.8 was released. The creator of Ruby made a lot of changes in the 1.8 version including WEBrick, Duck Typing, Ruby-Run, Open-Uri, StringIO, and other minor additions.

RubyGems was introduced to the public in 2004. Its birth also marked the start of more good things to happen.

Ruby took off in 2005 with the introduction of Ruby on Rails. The new framework had somewhat affected the flow of web development for the better. Ruby had always been the favorite choice in writing CGI scripts, but Ruby on Rails has managed to take it to the next level.

The Model-View-Controller structure of Ruby on Rails gives full concentration on convention over configuration that web application developers truly appreciate. People got hooked and the Ruby community displayed an immense fondness to the Rails framework. The positive response made Ruby popular.

In 2007, Ruby 1.8.6 was introduced to the world. During the said year, Mac OS X allowed the installation of Ruby programming language.

In 2008, version 1.8.7 was released. At this point in time, Ruby can be considered at the peak of success.

The development version of Ruby 1.9 started in December, 2007. It only got stabilized in the year 2011 with these notable changes: new hash syntax, more string formatting, improved file loading performance, new methods, new encoding support, enhanced speed, and many more.

In the early part of 2013, Ruby 2.0.0 was launched and offered stabilizing changes like never before. It introduced optimized garbage collection, safe monkey patching, built-in syntax documentation, keyword arguments, further speed improvements, and more.

On Christmas of 2013, Ruby 2.1.0 was introduced to the market. Although it only had minor changes, but the introduction of semantic versioning made version 2.1.0 more valuable than most versions of Ruby language.

On February 24, 2014, Ruby's 21st anniversary, the version 2.1.1

was introduced to the world. The new version focused on bug fixes and speed improvements. After 3 months, Ruby 2.1.2 was released. The latest version during that year was more stable than 2.1.1.

More stable versions of Ruby were released in the years that followed. Most of them only enhanced the features of the predecessor version of the Ruby language. It is possible that in the near future, a completely different version of Ruby language may appear.

Codes evaluation, Objects, Methods, Classes, and Instances

How Your Computer Evaluates the Ruby Codes

Ruby Objects

Ruby Methods

Ruby Classes

Ruby Instances

How Your Computer Evaluates the Ruby Codes

The Ruby interpreter, which is the programming language's main brain responsible for translating the written code or program, reads the program or code from left to right and top to bottom. It literally starts translating from first character of the first line down to the last character of the last line of the program.

If the interpreter encounters an error, it will stop executing or interpreting the rest of the codes and pops an error message regarding the mistake it encountered. It usually gives the line number of the error. The error could be improper use of constants, misspelled names of identifiers or variables, a violation of a certain rule, and others.

When you encounter an error message, you must be able to decipher and correct it. Often times, the errors are only misspelled words due to carelessness. Make sure to write your codes correctly and review them as you write. It is also best to assign variable names that are short, easy to remember, and relevant to the process or operation.

When writing your codes, make sure to follow a systematic, logical flow. For example, you want to present different values and would like to print the sum of those values in line ten. Your code must have the calculations somewhere before line ten, which should be between lines 1 and 9. Keep in mind that the interpreter evaluates the code one character at a time in each line.

Ruby Objects

The Ruby programming language regards the object as its heart. If you will go back to the previous statement regarding Ruby being an object-oriented language, you will see that Ruby treats all the data as an object. It controls the data like an object. There are a lot of object-oriented languages, but very few can be considered as true object-oriented language.

Ruby treats the data like object and places them in the center. Each object is different from each other because every one of them has their unique characteristics. Take a string as an example. It is an object with built-in characteristics, which give the string the ability to handle text.

Ruby Methods

A method defines the action that needed to be performed on the object. Most object-oriented programming languages have built-in object methods and definitions – Ruby has it too. To give you an idea about Ruby methods, take the method named `capitalize` as an example. It can be used for the Ruby class strings.

Take a look at this example:

```
1   samp1 = "you are great!"
```

The name "samp1" is a name of a variable (more about it on Chapter 3). The "=" sign means the variable has an assigned value. The string "you are great!" is the value assigned to variable samp1.

If you want the assigned value's first letter in uppercase, then you can add the method `capitalize` to convert the first character into a capital letter. This is how you add (or call) the method:

```
samp1.capitalize
```

To see the result, you can write a simple code like this:

```
1  #Sample program 1
2  samp1 = "you are great!"
3  puts samp1.capitalize
```

The method capitalize simply instructs the Ruby interpreter to turn the first character of the assigned value into a capital letter. The above code will give you this result:

```
You are great!
```

You should have noticed that when a method was called, it followed this pattern:

```
{{object name}}.{{method name}}
```

In the above sample, the object is a string (assigned to the variable samp1). If you use the method capitalize on a variable that does not contain a string value or the object is not a string, Ruby will pop an error message.

You can also create any method for any of your objects. Here is the way to do that:

```
def method_name
#Enter your code here
end
```

The hash sign # informs the Ruby interpreter that the line is not executable and merely placed there to act as a comment or reminder for the human user or programmer. Every time the Ruby interpreter encounters a line with a hash sign, it automatically skips the line.

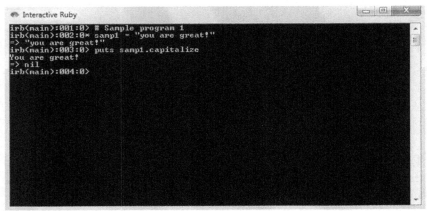

This is the screen of Interactive Ruby or irb.

This is the screen of Ruby online.

Ruby Classes

You can think of a class like a blueprint. It allows you to create a particular type of objects that you need for your program. You can also create methods that define the actions that you need the objects to do or accomplish.

Know that a class has a special property known as inheritance, which means shared traits or characteristics with a subclass or subclasses. You can view the Ruby inheritance as something similar to inheriting something from a parent. It is either you get biological attributes or properties – it is something that is passed down to the child or offspring.

To give a clearer explanation, think that there are parent, children, and grandparent classes. The children classes inherit the entire parent's or grandparent's attributes. In Ruby language, the grandparent class of the object is called superclass. Simply put, if you have an object that has a string attribute, your object inherits the "string class" properties. The parent class of your string class is the superclass of that string.

Important thing to keep in mind: the superclass of string, which instructs Ruby regarding the way to treat strings, is different from superclass of a string object.

Ruby Instances

To explain the Ruby class instances better, take a look at the recipe of apple pie. A class is similar to a recipe, which contains a list of different ingredients and the instructions on how to cook the dish. The moment you take out the cooked pie from the oven and sliced it, each slice may be considered as the instance of the class pie. Each slice of pie or instance is considered an object. You create an instance like this:

```
pie = SliceofApplePie.new
```

It is enough that you know something about how you computer evaluates the Ruby codes as well as the other things that were discussed in this subchapter. You will learn more about methods later on.

CHAPTER 2: INITIAL PREPARATIONS

RUBY INSTALLATION

Where to Get Ruby

Using a Code Editor

Ruby Styles

Important Notes to Remember on Ruby Syntax

Where to Get Ruby

Once again, here is the link to the site where you can download Ruby for free:

https://www.ruby-lang.org/en/

When you click the provided link, you will automatically access the downloadable Ruby programming language. Download the Ruby version that is suitable to your operating system. All you need to do is follow the instructions when downloading the right Ruby in your computer.

For the online version you can go to this link:

https://www.tutorialspoint.com/execute_ruby_online.php

It is recommended to get the 1.9.3 version or higher. Those who are using a later model of Linux or Mac unit, you should already have an installed Ruby in your unit.

Along the line that says `C:\Users\hp>` (this is the command prompt, see image below), when you type `ruby - v` you will see the version of Ruby installed in your computer. If you type `gem -v` next to the command prompt, you will see the version of RubyGems in your machine.

There are Ruby installations, particularly on Mac, that have restricted permissions and can hinder you to install gems. You need to upgrade your Ruby to be able to perform other tasks. If your machine comes with a restricted Ruby, you still need to re-install Ruby to gain full access and be able to install RubyGems.

Using Code Editor

You need to use a code editor to write the code or program. A code editor uses plain text with no styling or formatting. You can use the text editor like Notepad, Emacs, TextMate, and others. When using Ruby Interactive, you simply type in your codes directly on the screen. If you prefer using the online Ruby version, you can directly type in the codes or use a text editor and just transfer or paste your codes.

You can save your work when you use a text editor. You must choose a filename that can immediately give information about what the code or program needs to accomplish.

Take note that you must avoid using advanced text editors or word processor. They are intended for writing and not for coding. They often include whitespace or characters into the document that are invisible to the naked eye. Any unnecessary additions could lead to unexpected behavior of the program or even cause bugs.

Ruby Styles

The Ruby language follows a specific writing style that can create ease and convenience when writing and reading the Ruby codes.

You need to get used to these things immediately for your code to look pleasing to the eyes.

Set your text editor's tab to 2 spaces. Indenting can help make the program more readable. It is also easy to maintain the system if the code is presented nicely. Usually in a company, a team that created the program may not be the team assigned to maintain it. Coding the program in a nice, easy-to-read way can help shorten the time to fix it when there's a bug in the system.

A # sign that can be found at the start of a line means that everything after the hash sign within that same line is considered a comment. Comments also serve as notes or information that can help the programmers recall or know something about the program.

The entire system may have different sub-programs or modules. There are times when a programmer only needs to fix a certain module to repair the entire system.

When you initialize or define a file, method, or variable, it is recommended to always use snake_case formatting. The snake_case formatting uses lower case letters and separates each word with underscore.

```
1   # Naming a file
2   sample_of_snake_case_file.rb
3
4   # Assigning a variable
5   seventy = 70
6
7   # Defining a method
8   def sample_method
9     # write your set of codes
10  end
```

When you want to assign a value to a variable with no intention of changing the assigned value, you need to define it as constant. In Ruby, you must write constants in uppercases.

```
1   # Constant declaration
2   ONE = "one"
3   SIX = 6
```

When using do/end blocks, you can use { } if the entire expression can fit within a single line. If you don't have this symbol (|) in your keyboard, you can use this symbol (¦) – they are the same.

```
1   # Multi-line
2   [1, 2, 3].each do |i|
3       # do things
4   end
5
6   # Performs same thing in one line
7   [1, 2, 3].each { |i| # do things }
8
```

It is advisable to use CamelCase formatting when naming your classes. You are not allowed to use spaces in CamelCase. You need to keep in mind that you must capitalize the first letter of each word when naming your class.

```
1   # Class naming
2   class TheInitialClass
3   end
4
5   class TheOtherClass
6   end
```

For now, that's all you need to know to get started. If you want to know more about the Ruby styles in the future, you can click this link.

25

Important Notes to Remember on Ruby Syntax

There are important notes to remember when writing a Ruby programming code, and you need to remember them. Some of these notes may seem vague for now, but they will come in handy later as you advance.

The Ruby code ignores the tabs and spaces (the whitespace), except when you use spaces in strings to make them readable.

In Ruby programming, the newline characters and semicolons signify a statement ending. However, the presence of an operator, such as backslash or +, at the end of a statement indicates a continuation.

The names of the methods, constants, and variables are also known as the identifiers. Be careful when writing and using the identifiers for they are case sensitive. Most programmers encounter an error caused by the identifiers. Ruby treats the variable "num1" as something different from "Num1". When you assigned a value to num1 and tried to print Num1, you will get an error that says, "Uninitialized constant Num1." You need to check your code and make sure that you have written the variables or identifiers in their proper cases.

DOCUMENTATION, CLASSES, METHODS, AND MORE

Learning to Read Ruby Documentation

Module Name and Class Name

Methods

Learning to Read Ruby Documentation

If you are keen on becoming a programmer, then you need to develop a reading habit and take time to go through the programming language's documentation.

The Ruby language, like most well-liked programming languages, offers a wide array of standard libraries that are readily available at your disposal. However, there is a need to spend ample time to familiarize yourself with all the different methods and classes that are already available to use. For now, it is best to just know some of them as you learn the Ruby language.

Understand that you will be able to learn Ruby in 24 hours, but you need more time to become an expert. After reading this entire book, you should be able to do simple programming. Depending on your ability to grasp things, you may even do a short complex program later. You will be able to code something already after or even during each lesson.

Some developers prefer the term API (application programming interface) to refer to the programming language documentation. Below is a `String` class screenshot taken from www.ruby-doc.org (the official Ruby documentation source). Pay close attention to the encircled areas.

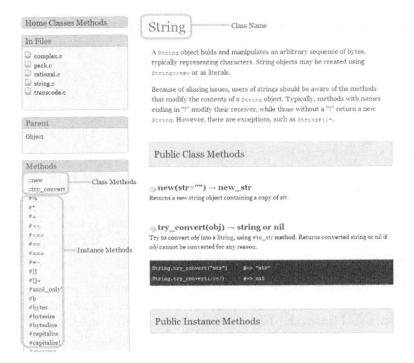

Module Name and Class Name

Looking at the image above, the class name is String. In some documentation you will notice a :: symbol to refer to a class name, just like in this one: `Encoding::Converter`. The symbol :: actually defines a namespace and create a distinction between Ruby classes. The symbol also serves as a way to separate classes from the others that happen to have the same name.

For example, you have ActiveRecord::Base and CurrentRecord::Base. Both have class named Base, but the only thing similar to both of them is their name. One is Base class in the module ActiveRecord and the other is a Base class in the module CurrentRecord.

When you open a particular class, you are provided with all the information regarding that class as well as the things that you are allowed to do. Look at the same figure above once more and take note that the side bar with the symbol :: has a different meaning – the name after the said symbol refers to the class method.

Methods

The methods that use # are instance methods (see figure above) and the methods that use : : are class methods. These symbols bear such meanings only for Ruby documentation. Remember that in actual Ruby code, the hash sign is used to indicate comment and the double colon sign is used to indicate namespace.

Using the same example, the String class, let us try to apply the class method String.new and String.try_convert. Take a look below:

```
irb :001 > p = String.new("pink")

=> "pink"
irb :002 > String.try_convert("blue")
=> "blue"
```

Now let us try instance methods. If you visit the Ruby documentation for String class and scroll down, you will see split method. Look at the sample below:

```
irb :001 > "the world is a stage".split
=> ["the", "world", "is", "a", "stage"]
```

Did you notice how the method was called out? When using class method, you state the name of the class first followed by the method and you need to enclose the object in parenthesis. When using instance method, you state the object followed by the method.

CHAPTER 3: START WITH THE BASICS

GETTING FAMILIAR WITH STRINGS, SYMBOLS, NUMBERS, AND NIL

Strings

Symbols

Numbers

Nil

Strings

A collection of characters in a sequence is usually called a string. A string can have double quotes (" ") or single quotes (' '), and you can use either format. But, you need to observe some basic rules in using them.

You have two options to choose from when you need to use quotes within the string. You can use the method that uses double-quotes or the method that uses single-quotes with escaping. Take a look at this:

```
1  # Sample1: Double quotes
2  "Elena said, 'You first.'"
3
4  # Sample2: Single quotes and escaping
5  'Elena said, \'You first.\' '
```

The escape character or backslash (\)informs that the quotes after it are just plain quote characters and should not be regarded as part of Ruby programming syntax.

You can use the double quotes for string interpolation. Look at the sample below:

```
irb :001 > num1 = 'seven'
=> "seven"

irb :002 > "I choose number #{num1}!"
=> "I choose number seven!"
```

You can try it on your irb to see the actual result.

When you need to work with strings, you can use string interpolation to merge your Ruby code. Keep in mind that you can only use double quotes for string interpolation to work. As time goes by, you will get familiar with this technique as you continue to further develop your Ruby programming skill.

Symbols

Basically, you use a symbol to serve as reference, especially if you don't want to print it on screen or manipulate it in any way. The Ruby symbols are commonly created via putting a colon before a word.

Numbers

There are numerous ways that you can present numbers in Ruby. Integer is a form of number that is considered the most basic. It is always whole number without decimal point. There is also something called float, which is a complex form and has a decimal point.

The examples of integers are 1, 3, 25, 100, 1058894, and so on. The examples of floats are 3.14, 1.83, 23.25974, and so on.

Nil

All programming languages must have means to present "nothing", and in Ruby language it is presented by nil. Something that has a nil value is totally empty or without any particular type. The best example to demonstrate this is a situation where there is an expected output but nothing is returned. Take a look at this:

```
irb :001 > puts "Hello, Ruby World!"
Hello, Ruby World!
=> nil
```

You can use the method puts to print out the string on your computer screen. As you can see from the above example, it returns nothing (this symbol => signifies return). You can see that it returned nil.

Is it possible to use .nil to know whether a particular entity nil? Take a look at the sample below:

```
irb :001 > "Hello, Ruby World".nil?
=> false
```

The irb returned "false" when .nil was added after the string.

A nil type provides importance when included in the "if statement" or other expression. Take a look at the sample below:

```
irb :001 > if nil
irb :002 > puts "Hello, Ruby World!"
irb :003 > end
=> nil
```

It did not print "Hello, Ruby World!" on the screen because it treated the statement or expression as a false condition. It did not read the next line because the condition is already false. But, if you will do this instead:

```
irb :001 > if 1
irb :002 > puts "Hello, Ruby World!"
irb :003 > end
Hello, Ruby World!
=> nil
```

It gets printed because the condition does not contain a false value. The value 1 is something and not "nothing". The next line was executed due to the fact that the `if` statement has provided a value `true`.

You will learn more about the `if` or conditional statements later.

RUBY OPERATIONS

Integers: Addition, Subtraction, Multiplication, and Exponentiation

Division and Modulo

Multiplying and Dividing Floats

Equality Comparison

Concatenation

Integers: Addition, Subtraction, Multiplication, and Exponentiation

In Ruby, it is fairly easy to do basic mathematical operations. You only need the operator + to add the integers together. Like this one:

```
irb :001 > 2 + 1
=> 3
irb :002 > 2 + 1 + 3 + 4
=> 10
```

Go and play more with integers on your irb. It is advisable to practice what you have learned to get familiar with the new Ruby function, command, or lesson.

When performing subtraction, use the - operator.

```
irb :001 > 2 - 1
=> 1
irb :002 > 11 - 1 - 3
=> 7
```

When performing multiplication, use the * operator.

```
irb :001 > 4 * 4 * 4
=> 64
irb :002 > 11 * 2
=> 22
```

When performing exponentiation, use the ** operator.

```
irb :001 > 6 ** 2
=> 36
irb :002 > 6 ** 3
=> 216
```

In line 1, the number 6 must be raised to two or should be squared. In line 2, the number 6 must be raised to three.

Division and Modulo

When performing division, use /.

```
irb :001 > 8 / 2
=> 4
```

There is modulo or remainder. It uses the % symbol. The answer that it gives is the remainder that it gathered from division. There may come a time when you need to use the exact remainder for your program to work and modulo can help a lot.

```
irb :001 > 25 % 4
=> 1
```

Multiplying and Dividing Floats

You can multiply floats and get an exact answer each and every time. Ruby will always return a float whenever you give a set of numbers to solve even if only one of them is in decimal form.

```
irb :001 > 3.75896 * 4
=> 15.03584
```

If you want to get the exact answer to a division problem that requires decimal point and no remainder, you need to use floats.

```
irb :001 > 11.0 / 4
=> 2.75
```

Keep this table of Ruby operators handy:

RUBY OPERATORS		
Sign	**Operand**	**Example**
+	Addition	5 + 2
-	Subtraction	10 - 3
*	Multiplication	7 * 1
/	Division	21 / 3
%	Modulo	215 % 8
**	Exponentiation	2 ** 5

Equality

There will be instances where you need to check whether the two objects have the same values. You can use the == operator to check the equality of two objects. The == operator compares the two objects on its left and right side. The result of such comparison will return either true or false. Most programming languages refer to both values as boolean.

You can try these examples on your irb and see the actual results with your own eyes.

```
irb :001 > 5 == 5
=> true

irb :002 > 0 == 5
=> false
```

You can also use the == operator on strings.

```
irb :001 > 'ruby' == 'ruby'
=> true

irb :002 > 'ruby' == "ruby"
=> true

irb :003 > 'ruby' == 'language'
=> false
```

What do you think will happen when you type the expressions below on your irb?

- '7' == 7

- '7' == 'seven'

The two sets of comparisons will both return false. In the first comparison, '7' has a different value from 7. The presence of quotes made the other 7 assume the value of a string, making them different from one another.

The next comparison, although being both strings, are still different from each other in the computer's point of view. Keep in mind that the computer only recognizes binary codes and '7' has a different binary code from 'seven'.

Concatenation

The concatenation in string is similar to addition of numbers. You add strings instead of numbers. You need the operator + to combine or join the strings.

```
irb :001 > 'ruby' + 'ruby'
=> "rubyruby"

irb :002 > 'ruby' + "ruby"
=> "rubyruby"

irb :003 > 'ruby' + 'language'
=> "rubylanguage"

irb :004 > 'ruby' + ' ' + 'language'
=> "ruby language"
```

If you look at line 4, you will notice that the addition of (' ') has created a gap between the two words as compared with the result in line 3.

Try to experiment and fool around more with your new discovery. It can help you get to know it better.

What do you think will happen if you have type '1' + '1' on your irb? If you think you will get 2, it makes sense but remember that you are dealing with strings (due to the presence of quotes). The correct answer would be "11".

What if you try to concatenate or join a string and an integer? Expect to get an error message.

TYPE CONVERSION AND OTHERS

Type Conversion

Arrays

Hashes

Puts vs. Returns

Type Conversion

Someday, you may encounter a situation wherein you must really combine `Fixnum` and `String`. For example, a user input '15' and the program needs to increment the number by 3. Ruby won't allow you to perform a mathematical operation between a string and a number. Even if you try, you will only see an error message.

Fortunately, there's a method that you can use to convert the `String` into `Fixnum` – it is called `to_i` method. It can be called in this manner:

`{string}.to_i`

```
irb :001 > '15'.to_i
=> 15

irb :002 > '15'.to_i + 3
=> 18
```

You can clearly see that the method `to_i` returned a `Fixnum`. The line 2 shows you that you can increment the value by 3 since it's been converted. You can perform other mathematical operations aside from addition. You can try it on your irb and explore other possibilities.

The other commonly used conversion operators are to_f, which converts an integer into a float, and to_s, which convert a number into a string. You can practice the different conversion operators and familiarize yourself. They are more useful than you think.

Arrays

If you need to organize an orderly list, then it is best to use an array. You can have floats, integers, strings, booleans, or other type of data in your list. It is easy to recognize an array in Ruby because it uses square brackets ([ ]). You need to make a list inside the brackets. Each element on the list is separated by a comma.

Here is an array of integers from 1 to 5:

```
irb :001 > [1, 2, 3, 4, 5]
=> [1, 2, 3, 4, 5]
```

You can access each array element through index. The index count always starts at zero. This is how an array with index should look like (the array is named "Sandwich"):

Sandwich

Tuna	[0]
Ham & Cheese	[1]
BLT	[2]
Pepperoni	[3]
Cheese Steak	[4]
Hamburger	[5]

If you want to access the second element in the array, then you need to call index 1.

Try to do this simple exercise on your own:

1. The name of your array is number.

2. It should contain the numbers 1 to 7.

3. Call the third element in the list.

Expect more exercises and program samples later. It is best to learn through examples and hone your skill via programming exercises. Know that there are different ways to tackle the problem and there could be more than one solution.

Going back to the simple programming exercise, you should have arrived at this answer:

```
irb :001 > number = [1,2,3,4,5,6,7]
=> [1,2,3,4,5,6,7]
irb :002 > number [2]
=> 3
```

There is another solution:

```
irb :001 > number = [1,2,3,4,5,6,7] [2]
=> 3
```

Keep in mind that the index always starts at 0.

Hashes

A hash comes with a set of key-value pairs and oftentimes it is also called a dictionary. It uses curly braces ({ }). In a key-value pair, a specific value is assigned to a key. The key is commonly represented by a symbol => that clearly points to the value.

```
irb :001 > {:monkey => 'eats banana'}
=> {:monkey => 'eats banana'}
```

The sample hash above is a one key-value pair. Like arrays, hashes can have multiple items separated by commas. You don't need to worry about having them in specific order.

```
irb :001 > {:one=>'I',:two=>'II',:three=>'III'}
=> {:one=>'I',:two=>'II',:three=>'III'}
```

What if you want to find out the Roman numeral of two? You can retrieve the information that you want by its key.

```
irb :001 > {:one=>'I',:two=>'II',:three=>'III'}[:two]
=> "II"
```

You can also write the above samples this way:

```
irb :001 > num= {:one=>'I',:two=>'II',:three=>'III'}
=> {:one=>'I',:two=>'II',:three=>'III'}
irb :002 > num [:two]
=> "II"
irb :003> num [:three]
=> "III"
```

When you write the code like in the sample above, you don't need to write the hash over and over again. All you need to do is write the hash name and the key. It is also easier to access the other keys as evident in line 3.

Puts and Return

Before we discuss all about puts and return, are you curious about the "=>" sign that you see in your Interactive Ruby or irb? The sign is called hash rocket, which is usually followed by expression that Ruby returns. Each time you type something in your irb, you are generating an expression.

Anything that can be evaluated is called expression. That being said, most of the things that you write in Ruby can be evaluated and considered expressions. In Ruby programming, an expression always returns something – even `nil` or an error message.

It is usual for new programmers, who don't have prior programming knowledge, of Ruby language to get confused with `puts` and `return`. The confusion arises from the misunderstanding caused by insufficient or misleading information.

When you call `puts` method in Ruby, you are giving an instruction to print something on the computer screen. Keep in mind that the expression does something and needs to return something. However, the returned value may not always be the performed action.

```
irb :001 > puts 'anything'
anything
=> nil
```

As you can see, the word 'anything' gets printed on the screen and returned a `nil`.

43

CHAPTER 4: RUBY VARIABLES

UNDERSTANDING VARIABLES

What's a Variable?

Reserved Words that Should not be Used as Variable Names

Assigning Value to a Variable

Simple Exercises

What's a variable?

A variable serves as a container in which you store the data that you need for your program. It is important to give each variable in your program code a unique and relevant name. It is also important that the variable name is easy to recall. The content of your variable may change depending on the program flow.

For example, you want a program that can add two numbers that can assume different values each time the program runs. You need to prepare a container for each number and also set up the mathematical function that must be applied between the containers. This way, the user doesn't need to edit the source code just to get the sum of the new set of numbers. It is also more convenient and efficient if the source program can automatically compute for the sum of the new set of numbers.

Do it like this:

total = first_number + second_number

The above representation is still better than doing it like this:

total = 1 + 2

In the second presentation, you need to change the value of the constants 1 and 2 into a new set of values each time you run the program to satisfy the requirements of the user. You actually need to alter the source code to achieve such feat, which is also too troublesome and inefficient.

You can use the variables or the data they contain throughout your program.

Reserved Words that Should not be Used as Variable Names

Below is the list of Ruby reserved words. You should not use these reserved words as variable or constant names when coding your program. Each word in the list has a specific function to perform.

while	Retry	for	break
and	ensure	or	unless
do	BEGIN	next	then
nil	end	redo	FALSE
undef	until	rescue	when
def	not	elsif	alias
class	in	return	TRUE
case	self	if	__FILE__
defined?	module	super	__LINE__
END	else		

If you encounter a syntax error, then it is possible that you inadvertently used a reserved word as your variable name.

Assigning Value to a Variable

Giving a variable its name is a grueling task for a programmer. When you give a variable its name, you need to come up with something unique and not a reserved word in Ruby. The name should be unique and should provide a short description regarding where it should be used or the reason for its existence.

You can assign a number or string to your variable. You use the equal sign (=) to assign the value. Don't mix up the signs '==' (which compares equality) and '='.

Remember that when you assign a value, the variable name is placed at the left side of the equal sign and the value is placed at the right side. Take a look at this one:

```
irb :001 > surname = 'Jackson'
=> "Jackson"
irb :002 > age = 17
=> 17
```

In the given sample, the variable surname has an assigned string value 'Jackson'. In line 2, the variable age has an assigned integer value 17. Each time you call or use a particular variable in your program, it will give you the value that it contains. If the value remains constant throughout the program, then your program will use the same value. Just to give you a heads up, there are cases where the value of your variable may change and you will know more about it later.

Looking at the given sample, your program will retrieve the value 'Jackson' each time you use the variable surname in your program. It will likewise retrieve the value 17 each time you use the variable age.

Try this simple exercise:

1. Assign 3 to variable a.

2. Assign 4 to variable b.

3. Assign 7 to variable c.

4. Get the sum of a, b, and c.

You should be able to come up with this answer:

```
irb :001 > a = 3
=> 3
irb :002 > b = 4
=> 4
irb :003 > c = 7
=> 7
irb :004 > a + b + c
=> 14
```

What if you are asked to assign the sum of a + b + c to variable d, instead of just getting the total? Your answer should look like this:

```
irb :001 > a = 3
=> 3
irb :002 > b = 4
=> 4
irb :003 > c = 7
=> 7
irb :004 > d =  a + b + c
=> 14
```

You can also re-assign the value of variables. Take a look at this:

```
irb :001 > a = 3
=> 3
irb :002 > c = 2
=> 2
irb :003 > c = a
=> ???
```

Can you guess the returned value for variable c? Even though it has an initial value of 2, it was replaced by the value that variable a contains. It will return 3. Try in on your irb and you will see.

You can practice more before you try the simple exercises below. Remember to try to do things on your own first before looking at the answer. You are trying to learn, so don't cheat!

Simple Exercises

You already know the different mathematical operators in Ruby, we will use them on the variables. You will see the answers at the end of the last task.

First task:

1. Assign 5 to variable num1.

2. Assign 3.55 to variable num2.

3. Assign 'Lucky' to variable word1.

4. Assign 'Sure' to variable word2.

5. Print num2.

6. Print word1.

Second task:

1. Assign 20 to variable a.

2. Assign 10 to variable b.

3. Assign 30 to variable c.

4. Get the sum of the three variables.

Third task:

1. Assign 20 to n1.

2. Assign 15 to n2.

3. Get the difference of n1 and n2, and assign it to variable dif.

Fourth task:

1. Assign 4 to m1.

2. Assign 7 to m2.

3. Print the product of m1 and m2.

Answer to the first task:

```
irb :001 > num1 = 5
=> 5
irb :002 > num2 = 3.55
=> 3.55
irb :003 > word1 = 'Lucky'
=> "Lucky"
irb :004 > word2 = 'Sure'
=> "Sure"
irb :005 > puts num2
3.55
=> nil
irb :006 > puts word1
Lucky
=> nil
```

Answer to the second task:

```
irb :001 > a = 20
=> 20
irb :002 > b = 10
=> 10
irb :003 > c = 30
=> 30
irb :004 > a + b + c
=> 60
```

Answer to the third task:

```
irb :001 > n1 = 20
=> 20
irb :002 > n2 = 15
=> 15
irb :003 > dif = n1 - n2
=> 5
```

Answer to the fourth task:

```
irb :001 > m1 = 4
=> 4
irb :002 > m2 = 7
=> 7
irb :003 > puts m1 * m2
28
=> nil
```

Consider this one as a special task. Try to do this on your own:

1. Assign 1 to d1.

2. Assign 2 to d2.

3. Assign 3 to d3.

4. Assign 4 to d4.

5. Assign 5 to d5.

6. Assign 20 to d6.

7. Get the quotient of d6 and d4.

8. Get the remainder of d6 and d3.

9. Assign d2 to d3.

10. Print d3.

11. Raise d5 to 2.

12. Print the sum of d2, d6, and d5.

USER INPUT AND VARIABLE SCOPE

User Input

Variable Scope

User Input

In the real world, the users are usually the ones who must input the needed data. Up until now, you are the only one who assigns the values or data that you need to include in your program. There is a thing called user input, wherein the user can personally type in the data that the program needs to satisfy a certain process or set of codes.

You can allow the user to type in their information by using the `gets` method. When you use `gets`, the program waits for the user to input the information that the program asks and to press the enter key afterwards. It's like this:

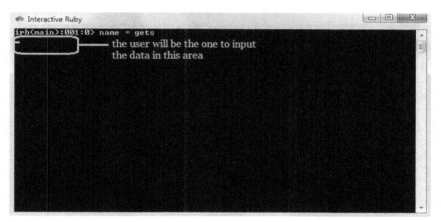

Let's say the user typed in Maria. The irb will display this result:

```
Interactive Ruby                                          ⌐ □ X
irb(main):001:0> name = gets
Maria
=> "Maria\n"
irb(main):002:0> _
```

Take a closer look at the image above. As you can see, Ruby returned the name that the user typed in and there's a '\n' next to that name. The '\n' is known as the newline character. If you don't want to see it as part of the typed user info, you can use chomp to chop it off. You can also use chomp after the string to eliminate the carriage return character that appears at the end.

```
Interactive Ruby                                          ⌐ □ X
irb(main):001:0> name = gets.chomp
Maria
=> "Maria"
irb(main):002:0>
```

Why do you need to use chomp? You need it to make the entry aesthetically appealing. Take a look at the two samples below:

```
irb :001 > name = gets
Maria
=> "Maria\n"
irb :002 > name + ' is pretty'
=> "Maria\n is pretty"
```

```
irb :001 > name = gets.chomp
Maria
=> "Maria"
irb :002 > name + ' is pretty'
=> "Maria is pretty"
```

Which one of the two is more appealing? It is definitely the second sample.

Variable Scope

A variable's scope determines the location of the available variable for use in the program. It is defined by where the creation or initialization of variable took place. A variable scope is defined by a piece of program, which follows a method invocation, called block. A method invocation is usually bordered with curly braces ({ }) or do/end. Bear in mind that not all do/end pairs constitute a block.

Suppose you have a file called extent.rb and you have the following code:

```
# extent.rb

ans = 7    #this variable initialization is done in
             the outer scope

4.times do |n|
  ans = 4 #do you think variable 'ans' is accessible
             in this inner scope?
end

puts ans
```

What would be the value of ans when printed? The value of ans would be 4. The variable ans was initialize in the outer scope and also available in the inner scope courtesy of the do/end block.

Here's another sample:

```
# extent.rb

ans = 7    #this variable initialization is done in
```

```
     the outer scope

4.times do |n|
   ans = 4
   rep = 8 #initialization is done in this inner
           scope
end

puts ans
puts rep
```

When you run the second program, you will get an error message that you have undefined method or local variable. It is because variable rep is not available in the outer scope, and it was only initialized in the inner scope. Ruby won't print the value of variable rep.

TYPES OF VARIABLES

Constants

Global Variables

Class Variables

Instance Variables

Local Variables

Constants

Constants are considered revered global variables because their lives remain constant in the entire existence of your program. When you declare your constants, you need to use capital letters in writing their names. Although most programming languages follow the rule of not changing the value of their constants, Ruby permits it. However, Ruby will give you a warning regarding the constant variable having a previous declaration.

Just because Ruby gives you absolute authority to change the value, it doesn't mean that you should change it on a whim. It is advisable that you keep the original value constant to avoid possible complications. You cannot declare constants in methods, and they are available to your application's scope the whole time.

Sample of constant declaration:

USE_THIS = 'Should be available all the time.'

Global Variables

You can use global variables in the entire program. Most Ruby programmers shy away from them for fear of facing unexpected complications when dealing with them. It always starts with a dollar sign ($) immediately followed by a variable name.

To illustrate further, say you want to calculate the area of different sizes of rectangles and would like to use a uniform width of 25 to all of the rectangles. You can declare: `$width = 25`.

All throughout the program, no matter which sub-module the program runs, you can reference `$width`. However, it is advisable not to change the value of your global variable even though Ruby permits it. If you change the value, you may only screw things up for another function or method that depends on the initial or original value of the variable.

Class Variables

The scope of a class variable is limited to the class they were defined or declared. The class variable name always starts with '@@'. Aside from the class itself, these variables are also accessible by class instances.

You need to initialize the class variables at the class level. Their values can be altered using instance or class methods. You can declare it like this: `@@length = 20`.

Instance Variables

The scope of instance variable is limited only to a certain instance of a class. The instance variable always starts with '@' immediately followed by the variable name. It is best not to use instance variables at this point in time, unless you fully grasp everything that you need to know about Ruby instance.

You can declare it this way: `@rem = 'Use me throughout the instance of this class'`

Local Variables

These variables comply with all scope boundaries. They are the most common or the usual variable type that you use for your program. The local variable does not need any special character before its name. You can declare it this way: `num1 = 20`.

CHAPTER 5: ALL ABOUT METHODS

WHAT ARE METHODS?

What are Methods?

Why do we Need Methods?

Default Parameters

Optional Parentheses

What are Methods?

When you begin to code complex or long programs, expect to have a module or sub-program that you need to execute over and over again within the whole program. Instead of writing that piece of code repeatedly, you can take advantage of the so called procedure in most programming languages. In Ruby programming, it is called method.

Before you can use a Ruby method, you need to define it first. You need to put def before the name of the method and affix end to signify the completion of a method. It is something like this:

```
def yo
  # the code for your method
end
```

Let us create a method named yo. We will also use a dummy file called yo.rb to contain the code.

```
# yo.rb

puts "hi"
puts "it's good to see you"
puts "hope you are happy"
puts "I'm glad you're fine"
```

As you can see, the code has a lot of puts. For the purpose of demonstrating how we can eliminate using a lot of puts, we will create a method to do that.

```
# yo.rb refactored

def yo(texts)
  puts texts
end

yo("hi")
yo("it's good to see you")
yo("hope you are happy ")
yo("I'm glad you're fine ")
```

It may appear impractical, but remember that the reason for doing this is to give you an idea regarding the advantage of using Ruby method. On the other hand, the program became more flexible than not having any method.

You can call the method when you type its name as well as pass the arguments. You also need to set a parameter when defining a method. You need a parameter when you have data in the method block's outer scope, and need to gain access to it within the scope of the method.

In the above sample, the parameter is '(texts)'. You place the parameter next to the method name when you define it. If the method does not need to gain access to any data outside the method's scope, then there's no need to set a parameter.

You can give any name to your parameter, but it is advisable to give meaningful and explicit names to your parameters. In this case, the parameter was named texts because the method yo needs to handle some texts. The pieces of data that are sent to a method are called arguments, which can be modified or employed to send back a specific result.

Looking at the sample above, the arguments were passed to a method when it was called. In the example, the words or arguments that were passed into the method were assigned to texts. You can use them according to your program's requirements, but make sure to use them within the method. You cannot reference `texts` outside the `yo` method block.

When Ruby executes the line `yo("hi")`, the string 'hi' becomes the argument that gets assigned to `texts` parameter. The method will perform the things that it needs to do with the presented argument. In this case, it needs to print it on screen.

One of the benefits of having a method is the ability to create some changes in one area that paves way to an astounding effect. Suppose you need to add a period at the end of each argument that must be sent to the method. It is tedious to add the period manually to each argument. You simply need to make some alterations in the method block. See the altered method below:

```
# yo.rb refactored

def yo(texts)
  puts texts + '.'   #the change is highlighted for
                     you
end

yo("hi")
yo("it's good to see you")
yo("hope you are happy ")
yo("I'm glad you're fine ")
```

When you run the code, each line will have a period at the end. If you have so many lines to alter, then doing it manually will definitely eat a lot of time. Having a method that will do it in one go is definitely the best option.

Default Parameters

When defining your method, you may want to structure the method that you will use to make sure that it will always work. We will use the same `yo` method as an example, but we will restructure it to give a clear view of what a default parameter does.

```
# yo.rb refactored once more
```

```
def yo(texts='hello')
  puts texts + '.'
end

yo()
yo("hi")
yo("it's good to see you")
yo("hope you are happy ")
yo("I'm glad you're fine ")
```

When you run the code, you will see that yo() prints 'hello.' on the screen. It's because the program has provided a default parameter. Remove yo() and Ruby will not print 'hello.' on the screen.

Optional Parentheses

You can remove the parentheses if you want. You can write the sample code above like this:

```
# yo.rb refactored once more

def yo(texts='hello')
  puts texts + '.'
end

yo
yo "hi"
yo "it's good to see you"
yo "hope you are happy"
yo "I'm glad you're fine"
```

Compare the two styles, which one do you prefer? Reading Ruby codes can be quite tricky. It is advisable to use parenthesis to create some distinctions, although it is up to you to go with the style that you find more comfortable to write.

MUTATING THE CALLER AND MORE ON PUTS AND RETURN

Mutating the Caller

Another Dose of Puts and Return

More on Return

Mutating the Caller

There are times when the argument can be changed permanently as the program calls a method. It is called mutating the caller. If you can remember, the method arguments are scope within the method block and they are not made available outside that scope. Look at this example:

```
def some_method(digit)
  digit = 7 #the method returned this implicitly
end

ran = 2
some_method(ran)
puts ran
```

Looking at the sample code above, you can see that ran is passed in to the method named some_method. Within the said method, the value of ran is assigned to digit, which is within the scope of the method block. The variable digit is reassigned with the value '7'. Do you think this will affect the value of ran, which is 2?

The answer is no. The value of ran will remain unchanged because variable digit is scoped within the method level. This proves that methods cannot change or influence the value of the arguments passed in to them. However, there is an exemption to the rule. There are actions that can be performed to mutate the caller and change or modify the variables outside the scope of the method.

We will use array in the sample code. We will discuss more about arrays later. Let us assign an array to variable list and use the file named transform.rb:

```
# Sample of a method that permanently modifies its
argument
# transform.rb

list = [1, 2, 3]

def transform(array)
  array.pop
end

puts "Before mutation: #{list}"
transform(list)
puts "After mutation: #{list}"
```

You can also use `p` instead of `puts`, and see the difference. The variable list has been permanently altered when it passed the method `transform` (you can name it mutate if you want) even though list is not within the scope of the method. This is due to `.pop` method, which mutates the caller. `pop` removed the last digit in the array.

Now let us try to use a method that does not transform the value of variable list.

```
# Sample of a method where there's no modification
even though a method is called
# transform.rb

list = [1, 2, 3]

def unchanged(array)
  array.last
end

puts "Before mutation: #{list}"
unchanged(list)
puts "After mutation: #{list}"
```

When you run the code, you will see that the before and after mutation contain the same value of array list. The `.last` method does not intend to change or mutate the argument.

You need to memorize the ruby documentation or at least keep it handy in order to know the methods that can help mutate the caller. The link was already given to you in the previous chapter. Here it is again if you missed it: www.ruby-doc.org.

Another Dose of Puts and Return

By this time, you should be well acquainted with puts, how about return? Know that in Ruby, each method naturally returns an evaluated result of the latest executed line. Let us take this sample:

```ruby
# transform.rb

list = [1, 2, 3, 4, 5]

def transform(array)
  array.pop
end

p "Before mutation: #{list}"
transform(list)
p "After mutation: #{list}"
```

It should look like this on your irb:

```
Interactive Ruby
irb(main):001:0> # transform.rb
irb(main):002:0* list=[1,2,3,4,5]
=> [1, 2, 3, 4, 5]
irb(main):003:0> def transform(array)
irb(main):004:1>   array.pop
irb(main):005:1> end
=> :transform
irb(main):006:0> p "Before mutation: #{list}"
"Before mutation: [1, 2, 3, 4, 5]"
=> "Before mutation: [1, 2, 3, 4, 5]"
irb(main):007:0> transform(list)
=> 5
irb(main):008:0> p "After mutation: #{list}"
"After mutation: [1, 2, 3, 4]"
=> "After mutation: [1, 2, 3, 4]"
irb(main):009:0>
```

As you can see, the whole array gets printed before the mutation and number 5 is already missing from the list after the mutation. The method pop has removed the last entry in the array list. When transform(list) is called, the program returns the number 5. Simply put, when using the method pop it returns the last element that it has eliminated.

More on Return

Let us use the file named ret.rb for our sample code.

```
# ret.rb

def added(num)
  num + 2
end

ret_val = added (3)
puts ret_value
```

The program intends to save the returned value of the method added in a variable called ret_val. We need to print ret_val on the screen to clearly see its content (your irb will show the returned value). The program should print 5 on the screen because it is the value that the method returned.

Even if you write the code this way:

```
# ret.rb

def added(num)
  return num + 2
end

ret_val = added (3)
puts ret_value
```

You will still get the same output. What do you think will print if you have this code:

```
# ret.rb

def added(num)
  return num + 2
  num + 5
end

ret_val = added (3)
puts ret_value
```

The program above should still give 5, the number the program instructed it to return.

When you put or include a `return` in the middle of the method, it only returns the assessed result of `num + 2`, which is 5. The next line will not be executed.

Take note that you don't need to write the reserved word `return` just to make the method return something – it is a feature of Ruby programming.

CHAINING METHODS AND ARGUMENTS

Chaining Methods

Methods as Arguments

Chaining Methods

You already know that each method returns something, and you can also chain the methods together. It can give you the ability to write concise and efficient codes.

Suppose you have this method:

```
def add_four(num)
   num + 4
end
```

The method above will return the value incremented by 4. When you add these lines below the method:

```
add_four(3)   #returns 7
add_four(4)   #returns 8
add_four(5)   #returns 9
add_four(6)   #returns 10
```

The lines above will just return their corresponding value because there's no instruction to print them on screen. Remember that when you see this sign '=>' when you hit the 'enter button' while on irb, it means that the entry next to it is a returned value.

When you include this line:

```
add_four(3).times { puts 'Print 7 times'}
```

You are calling .times method on add_four(3)'s returned value, which is 7. When the line is executed it will print this on screen:

```
Print 7 times
Print 7 times
Print 7 times
Print 7 times
Print 7 times
Print 7 times
```

66

```
Print 7 times
=> 7
```

The last line indicates the returned value of 7, which tells us that Ruby allows the programmer to keep chaining method calls as long as needed.

Take a look at this:

```
"I am here".length.to_s        #returns "9" (converted
                                into a String)
```

The `length` method returns an integer, and `to_s` was called to convert it into a string. Take note that spaces are included in the length of the string – one space is equal to one character.

Let us modify the `add_four` method and write this code:

```
def add_four(num)
  puts num + 4
end
```

We use `puts` to print the incremented value on the screen, instead of merely having the value returned. Do you think the code below would work?

```
add_four(4).times { puts "What will happen?" }
```

When you run the code, you will get this error message:

```
NoMethodError: undefined method 'times' for
nil:NilClass
```

Ruby flashed the error message because somewhere along the line, it encountered a `nil` and it does not have any capability to respond to a `.times` method.

Let us take it step by step and run only this code:

```
add_four(4)
```

It will give this output:

```
8
=> nil
```

It prints the incremented value on screen, but notice that the returned value is nil. It is because puts always returns nil. Take another look at the code of the method. The last expression is puts n + 4 and the reason why nil is the returned value. It is no longer possible to keep chaining methods because the add_four method has a returned value nil.

Remember this: the chained call will break down if there's an exception or an expression returns a nil anywhere along the chain. To fix the code, that is to prevent the chain from breaking down, you can do this:

```
def add_four(num)
   nnum = n + 4
   puts nnum
   nnum
end
```

The new code will also return the printed value on the screen because nnum is the method's last expression.

Another important reminder: Ruby lets you take a glimpse on the value that is being returned. If the returned value is in quotes, that means it is a string. If you need the returned value to be an integer, then convert it immediately into an integer by calling .to_i.

Example:

```
num = gets.chomp
num2 = num + 6
```

When you type the code above on your irb it will look like this:

```
irb :001 > num = gets.chomp
5
=> "5"
irb :002 > num2 = num + 6
```

When you hit 'enter' after the last expression you will get this error message:

```
TypeError: no implicit conversion of
Fixnum into String
```

The error occurred because you cannot add two elements of different types. As you can see, the num = gets.chomp returned "5". It returned a string (remember the presence of quotes). You need to convert it into an integer in order to perform a mathematical operation.

Look at this:

```
irb :001 > num = gets.chomp.to_1
5
=> 5
irb :002 > num2 = num + 6
=> 11
```

That's why Ruby is a cool language. Once you have learned the principles, you will see that it is much easier to learn than other similar programming languages.

Methods as Arguments

You are already familiar with methods and how they are called. Take a look at these simple samples to explore it further. Let us use subtract and add as method names and call them.

```
def subtract(num1, num2)
  num1 - num2
end

def add(num3, num4)
  num3 + num4
end
```

We will assume that the variables are integers. Keep in mind that Ruby implicitly returns the last expression in the method. In this case, we don't need to worry about the type of values that Ruby will return since each method only has one line.

We will use 100 and 60 for both methods:

```
subtract(100, 60)    # returns 40
=> 40
add(100, 60)         # returns 160
=> 160
```

Now, we will create another method that we will name multiply. We will pass subtract(100, 60) and add(100, 60) as arguments to multiply method.

```
def multiply(num5, num6)
   num5 * num6
end

multiply(add(100,60), subtract(100, 60))
```

The last expression will return 6,400. You can also type complex expression like this one:

```
add(subtract(100, 60), multiply(subtract(10, 5),
add(25, 5)))
=> 190
```

Let us dissect each part to see if the answer is right.

190 = (100-60) + ((10-5) * (25+5))
190 = (40) + ((5) *(30))
190 = 40 + 150
190 = 190

Remember that the open parenthesis in the beginning must always have a corresponding close parenthesis. It is advisable to use parenthesis to group things together and see the ones that need to be processed first. You can also prevent confusion when you use parenthesis and make your code readable and pleasing to the eye.

Try the sample codes on your own and practice more if you want.

CHAPTER 6: FLOW CONTROL

CONDITIONALS

Comparison Operators

Conditionals

Comparisons and Boolean Value

Now we get to the meaty part of Ruby programming. You must have noticed that there are a lot of samples in this book. It is easy to learn any programming language if you can see different program samples. It is also easier to explain things if there are program samples that serve as guide than just telling how a certain program works or what it does.

You can try the codes for practice and then do them without relying on your notes to see how much you have learned. It is understandable that you won't be able to memorize everything in the Ruby documentation and it is advisable to take it a step at a time. You will definitely learn how to create a Ruby program in one day, but you need ample time to be an expert Ruby programmer.

The programmers that you know took a year or more to really master the syntax and flow of a certain programming language. They may only need a few hours to learn a new language, but the mastery will take a lot of time. In fact, you could be better than most of them when they started.

Before we get to conditionals, let us take a detour to the different comparison operators.

Comparison Operators

The comparison operators can help check whether each presented condition is true or false. The comparison operators are different from mathematical operators. The comparison operators do not

71

give exact solution to a mathematical problem. They exist for the purpose of verifying the truthfulness or falsehood of a certain expression. Either true or false, the data will need to fulfill a particular instruction.

Here is the comparison, equality, and logical operators table:

Comparison, Equality, and Logical Operators		
Sign	**Meaning**	**Example**
==	equal to	6 +1==7
!=	not equal to	4!=5+1
<	less than	20<23
<=	less than or equal to	7<=5+a
>	greater than	30>18
>=	greater than or equal to	5>=5-a
&&	and	num ==4 && num.even?
||	or	num == 3 || num == 6
!	not	!(7 ==7) =>False

Remember that '==' is different from '=', as explained in the previous chapter.

Conditionals

When you write a program, it is only natural that you want the data to arrive at the right decision. You want the data to do what is right on the given circumstances. In the world of programming, it is known as conditional flow. How can you make the data choose the right thing to do? You will need some help from conditionals.

A conditional can be considered a fork or several forks in your path. The conditionals can lead the data to the right path depending on the presented or defined parameters. The conditionals are formed using comparison operators and `if` statements.

We will use the file named `condition.rb` for this program:

```
irb :001 > # condition.rb

irb :002 > puts "Enter a number"
Enter a number
=> nil
irb :003 > num = gets.chomp.to_i
3
=> 3
irb :004 > if num == 1
irb :005 >     puts "Num is 1"
irb :006 > elsif num == 2
irb :007 >     puts "Num is 2"
irb :008 > elsif num == 3
irb :009 >     puts "Num is 3"
irb :010 > else
irb :011 >     puts "Num is not recognized"
irb :012 > end
Num is 3
=> nil
```

To get an input number from a user, it is necessary to use `gets`. We add `.chomp` to get rid of the cartridge return character. We also use `.to_i` to convert the string into an integer. The `if` statement uses the reserved words `if`, `elsif`, `else`, and `end`.

Run the given code three times more and make sure to follow these instructions:

1. Run the code for the second time and enter number 1. Press enter.

2. Run the code for the third time and press number 2. Hit enter.

3. Run the code for the fourth time, type in any number greater than 3.

You can repeat the third instruction again and again to review the effect.

The code is actually checking the entered number against the options that the program has provided. It checks whether the number is equal to any of the available options. If the number is not equal to any of the number in the provided options, the program will print that the number is not recognized.

It is safe to say that this program has effectively controlled the flow via setting conditionals.

See more samples below to familiarize yourself with the `if` statements:

```
# Sample 1
if number == 7
  puts "Number is seven."
end

# Sample 2
if x == 5
  puts "x is five"
elsif x == 4
  puts "x is four"
end

# Sample 3
z = gets.chomp.to_i
If z.between?(1,5)
    puts "Number is between 1 and 5"
else
    puts "Number is more than 5"
end
```

```
# Sample 4
if y == 7
  puts "y is 7"
else
  puts "y is not 7"
end

# Sample 5: you need to add "then" when using a one-
liner
if w == 6 then puts "w is six" end
```

Ruby is indeed an expressive language. It allows the programmer to append the `if` statement at the end. Take Sample 1 for instance. The code could also be written like this:

```
puts "Number is seven" if number == 7
```

You can also use `unless`, which is a Ruby reserved word. It is quite tricky to use if you are used to using the `if` statement – `unless` is the exact opposite of `if` statement. You can use it this way:

```
puts "Number is NOT 7" unless x == 7
```

Try to do this on your own:

1. Use the variable num and get the input from user.

2. If the user input is between 1 and 10, print "The digit is between 1 & 10".

3. If the user input is between 11 and 20, print "The digit is between 11 & 20".

4. If the user input is more than 20, print "The digit is more than 20".

You must try not to look at the answer as you write your code. This coding problem is a good programming exercise.

```
irb :001 > num = gets.chomp.to_i
8
=> 8
irb :002 > if num.between?(1, 10)
irb :003 >    puts "The digit is between 1 & 10"
irb :004 > elsif number.between?(11, 20)
irb :005 >    puts "The digit is between 11 & 20"
irb :006 > else
irb :007 >    puts "The digit is more than 20"
irb :008 > end
The digit is between 1 & 10
=> nil
```

Comparisons and Boolean Value

This section will give you more information regarding the comparison operators and help you manage complex conditional statements. You need to remember that the only thing that comparison operators return is boolean value. The boolean value is either true or false – it does not give any other response.

Let us discuss 6 of the comparison operators and the meaning of each. The remaining comparison operators will be discussed in the next subchapter.

1. The less than symbol (<) – the value on the left of the symbol must be lower than that on the right side.

Example:

```
irb :001 > 76 < 80
=> true
irb :002 > 80 < 76
=> false
```

2. The greater than symbol (>) – the value on the left of the symbol must be higher than that on the right side.

Example:

```
irb :001 > 100 > 80
=> true
irb :002 > 100 > 200
=> false
```

3. The less than or equal to symbol (<=) – the value on the left of the symbol must be lower than or equal to the value on the right side of this particular comparison operator.

Example:

```
irb :001 > 4 <= 5
=> true
irb :002 > 6 <= 5
=> false
```

4. The greater than or equal to symbol (>=) – the value on the left of the symbol must be higher than or equal to the value on the right side of this comparison operator.

Example:

```
irb :001 > 5 >= 7
=> false
irb :004 > 7 >= 7
=> true
irb :005 > 7 >= 6
=> true
```

5. The equal to operator (==) – the value on both sides of the operator must be equal. Since we've been using this for a while now, you must be familiar with it already.

Example:

```
irb :001 > 7 == 7
=> true
irb :002 > 7 == 3 + 4
=> true
irb :003 > '7' == 7
=> false
```

The last line in the sample is a sort of reminder that you need to compare two of the same data type. At first glance, '7' and 7 are indeed the same, but they have different data types. One is string while the other one is an integer — they are still different from one another.

6. The not equal to operator (!=) — the value on both sides of the operator must be not be equal — the complete opposite of equal to operator.

Example:

```
irb :001 > 7 != 8
=> true

irb :002 > 7 != 7
=> false

irb :003 > 34 != 43
=> true
```

Try to determine the boolean value of each expression:

1. (40 - 20) > 25

2. (10 + 17) == 2**10

3. 1**10 <= 2

4. 20 * 4 >= -20

5. 81 != 9**2

6. (30 - 10) < 35

7. (20 + 7) == 2**4

8. 14 <= 7 + 7

9. 20 * 4 >= 40

10. 100 != 10**2

COMBINING EXPRESSIONS

Table for the Final Boolean Value

Combining Expressions

Ternary Operator

Table for the Final Boolean Value

Before we start combining expressions, take a look at the table below:

Logical (Boolean) Operators	Final Answer
|| (or)	
False || False	FALSE
False || True	TRUE
True|| False	TRUE
True || True	TRUE
&& (and)	
False && False	FALSE
False && True	FALSE
True && False	FALSE
True && True	TRUE
! (not)	
! False	TRUE
! True	FALSE

This table can guide you in finding the correct final answer for the presented expressions. You will use it as reference when combining expressions. The logical operators compare the expressions on both sides of a particular operator and give result in boolean values. There are three logical operators that you need to remember: and (&&), or (| |), and not (!). Keep the table handy all the time.

Combining Expressions

By now, the conditional flow should be clear to you. If it's still a bit vague, it is best to go over the lesson one more time.

You can also combine multiple conditional expressions to create a scenario that is more specific. You can use && and | | operators.

1. The "and" operator (&&) – the expressions to the left and to the right of the operator should be both true to get a true boolean response or result.

The logical operator && checks if the expressions on either side of the operator are true and true, true and false, or false and false. The final answer depends on the condition of the statements or expressions.

Example:

```
irb :001 > (7 == 7) && (4 == 4)
=> true

irb :002 > (7 == 5) && (3 == 3)
=> false

irb :002 > (8 == 7) && (9 == 10)
=> false
```

2. The "or" operator (| |) – the expressions to the left or to the right of the operator should be true to get a true boolean response or result. That is, at least one expression is true for the entire statement to be true.

The logical operator | | checks if the expressions on either side of the operator are true or true, true or false, or false or false.

Example:

```
irb :001 > (8 == 8) || (11 == 11)
=> true

irb :002 > (3 == 12) || (100 == 100)
=> true

irb :002 > (9 == 5) || (15 == 25)
=> false
```

3. The "not" operator (!) – the operator inverts the boolean value of a particular expression. When a particular expression is true, adding ! operator will make it false. When a particular expression is false, adding ! operator will make it true.

Example:

```
irb :001 > !(4 == 4)
=> false

irb :002 > !(5 == 6)
=> true
```

When you are combining expressions, it is best to use parenthesis to group the expressions. This makes it more readable. It also helps the computer to accurately understand your objective. It will evaluate the parenthesis in the usual algebraic order.

Ruby follows the so called order of precedence when evaluating the multiple expressions. Here is the order:

1. Comparison: <=, <, >, >=

2. Equality: ==, !=

3. Logical 'and': &&

4. Logical 'or': ||

Take a look at this:

```
if a && b || d
  # do something
end
```

In the sample above, the first one to be executed is a `&&` b. If the expression is `true`, then Ruby will execute the `# do something` next. If a `&&` b returns `false`, then d will get a chance to get evaluated.

If d returns `true`, the next line gets evaluated. If d also returns `false`, then the program will leave the `if` statement.

Ternary Operator

The ternary operator is a common idiom in Ruby language that creates fast `if/else` statement because it has the capability to write it all in a single line.

The ternary operator uses these symbols: `?` and `:` .

Examples:

```
irb :001 > true ? "this is okay" : "this is bad"
 => "this is okay"

irb :001 > false ? "this is it" : "this is not it"
 => "this is not it"
```

How does it work? The computer first evaluates the expression on the left of `?` . If the said expression is true, the computer executes the code on the immediate right of the `?`. If the expression on the left of the `?` is false, then the computer executes the code on the right of the `:`.

The ternary operators will definitely come in handy, especially when you have become more familiar with `if` statements. You can always practice your coding skills on your irb if you are unsure of how a certain command works. Practice makes perfect and you already have all the tools that can help you develop your skill.

CASE STATEMENT

Case Statement

Exercises

Case Statement

A case statement bears similarities with an if statement, only with interface that is slightly different.

You will use the reserved words case, when, else, and end when working with case statements.

When creating a case, the first thing you need to do is define a case and then evaluate its value as well as the process to complete if a particular case is true. To give a clearer presentation, let us create a file called case_sample.rb to see how case statements work.

```
# case_sample.rb

sample = 3

case sample
when 3
  puts "The answer is 3"
when 2
  puts "The answer is 2"
when 1
  puts "The answer is 1"
else
  puts "There's no answer"
end
```

The code above is sort of a modified if statement. You can also do it this way:

```
# case_sample.rb (other version)

sample = 3

ans = case sample
when 3
```

```
    "The answer is 3"
when 2
    "The answer is 2"
when 1
    "The answer is 1"
else
    "There's no answer"
end

puts ans
```

If you want to get an input from the user, then you can write the code like this:

```
# case_sample.rb (another version)

sample = gets.chomp.to_i

case sample
when 3
    puts "The answer is 3"
when 2
    puts "The answer is 2"
when 1
    puts "The answer is 1"
else
    puts "There's no answer"
end
```

Your code appears more structured and readable when you use `case` statement. It is also easy to modify and debug.

You also need to remember to always be careful when writing or reading the Ruby codes. Know if the returned value is a string or integer and see how you can convert them if your statements or expressions are asking for the same types of data. Review the different signs or symbols as well as the operators that Ruby uses.

Exercises

It's time to practice what you have learned. Can you tell the boolean value of the expressions below? If you have doubts, you can type the expressions on your irb to verify your answer.

Task 1:

1. (30 * 5) >= 150
2. !(4>5) == (5==4+1)
3. 76 < 80
4. (44*2) > 100
5. 100**2 < 10**10

Task 2

Write a program for a method named try that contains a string argument. You need to code the string in lower cases, but it should print it in all caps. It should print it on screen. You can refer to the Ruby documentation to help you.

Task 3

Write a program that asks the user to input a number between 1 and 20. If the input number is between 1 and 5, print "The number is small". If the input number is between 6 and 15, print "The number is okay". If the input number is between 16 and 20, print "The number is awesome". You need to use case statement.

If you think task 3 is a bit difficult to do, then don't touch it – for now. You still need to practice your case statement a bit more to get the hang of it.

CHAPTER 7: ITERATORS AND LOOPS

SIMPLE LOOP

What is a Loop?

Creating a Simple Loop

Controlling the Loop

What is a Loop?

There are times when a certain program works best with a loop. What is a loop? There is a loop when a piece of code is being executed repeatedly within a specified number of repetitions or until a particular condition has been satisfied. You can write a code that instructs Ruby to repeat a particular segment or module in your program instead of writing the same code over and over again.

This chapter will cover the different Ruby loops and they are `loop`, `for` loops, `while` loops, and `do/while` loops.

To give you an idea about loops, here is a simple calculator program written in plain English.

```
#Calculator program for two numbers using while loop

while the user needs the program, do this:
    display on screen: Choice 1 - add
    display on screen: Choice 2 - subtract
    display on screen: Choice 3 - multiply
    display on screen: Choice 4 - divide
    display on screen: Choice 5 - end

#ask the user for the math operation to try

    if choice is 1:
        get the first number
        get the second number
        add the numbers
```

86

```
        display the result on screen

if choice is 2:
    get the first number
    get the second number
    subtract the 2nd number to the 1st number
    display the result on screen

if choice is 3:
    get the first number
    get the second number
    multiply the numbers
    display the result on screen

if choice is 4:
    get the first number
    get the second number
    perform division
    display the result on screen

if choice is 5:
    end the loop

Display a thank you message onscreen
END PROGRAM
```

As long as the user needs to use the program, it continues to present the user with the different choices such as add, subtract, multiply, divide, or end the program. Each choice has a separate module. The computer will continue to execute the code within the module as long as the user chooses that particular number or mathematical operation. The loop goes on until the user has decided to terminate the program by choosing 5.

The loop can go on for as long as you want and it can also end abruptly – it all depends on the objective or requirements of the program.

A Simple Loop

There is a keyword called `loop` in Ruby that takes a block denoted by `do ... end` or `{ ... }`. It is the easiest way to generate a loop in Ruby. A `loop` will run the code non-stop within the specified block until you have decided to stop it by simultaneously pressing ctrl and c on your keyboard or if you have included a break statement in your code.

Try to run this on your irb:

```
# sample_loop.rb

loop do
  puts "You will see this non-stop" # this will keep
      printing non-stop unless you hit Ctrl and c
      on your keyboard"
end
```

When you run the sample code above you will see this continuously running on your screen:

```
You will see this non-stop
You will see this non-stop
You will see this non-stop
You will see this non-stop
You will see this non-stop
You will see this non-stop
You will see this non-stop
You will see this non-stop
IRB::Abort: abort then interupt!  #this message will
appear when you have decided to hit the keys that
will break the loop
```

Controlling the Loop

It is not advisable to use the loop without using a break statement within the block. The infinite loop will eventually crash your system.

Look at this example:

```
# the_helpful_loop.rb

x = 0
loop do
  x = x + 1   # in the future, you can also write it
              this way: x += 1. For now, let us
              stick to the usual.
  puts x
```

```
    break  # this stop the execution and stop the loop
  end
```

The code above will only print '1' on the screen. The loop stops immediately because of the `break` statement in the code. Understand that break will only stop the loop and not the entire program. If there are lines that still need to be executed after the loop block with a `break` statement, the execution will continue according to the instructions of the program.

Now, let us try to print all the even numbers from 1 to 10 using `loop` statement.

```
# sample_loop.rb

z = 0
loop do
  z += 2
  puts z
  if z == 10
    break  # this will stop the loop
  end
end
```

The output will look like this:

As you can see from the above sample, the `break` statement was not immediately executed until z == 10. The `break` took effect when the `if` statement evaluated to true and executed the code within block.

You can use the same program to trace the odd numbers, but it is quite tricky. You need to print '1' first and you need to execute it outside the loop. You also need to change the `if` statement that contains the `break` statement. Before you look at the answer try to write the code on your own. You will know the answer later. First, let us look at another sample program.

Looking at the same program, you can also skip a particular even number and prevent it from being printed on screen. You can do this:

```ruby
# sample_loop_modified.rb

z = 0
loop do
  z += 2
  if z == 4
    next    # skips the next line if the number is 4
  end
  puts z
  if z == 10
    break   # this will stop the loop
  end
end
```

Check this out:

As you can see, number 4 is not printed because the computer skipped the printing process for that number. The execution only resumed on the loop's next iteration.

You can use break and next to other loop construct, aside from loop. They are regarded as Ruby's essential loop control concepts.

When you combine them with Ruby conditionals, you can start creating simple codes that bear interesting behavior.

Going back to the previous challenge, your code should look like this:

```
z = 1
puts z
loop do
   z += 2
   puts z
   if z == 11
     break   # this will stop the loop
   end
end
```

If you have initialized your variable z to 1 and still used z == 10 in your program, you must have encountered an infinite loop and presses ctrl and c just to stop it. What went wrong?

You need to initialize your variable z to 1 and increment it by 2 to get the odd numbers. If you use z == 10, then the loop won't really stop because z will never be equal to 10. Remember that you always add 2 to the current value of z to make all the odd numbers come out. You can also use z == 9 if you don't want to go beyond 10.

THE DIFFERENT LOOPS

While Loop

Until Loop

Do/While Loop

For Loop

While Loop

The `while` loop tells the computer to keep executing the code as long as the `while` statement or boolean expression returns `true`. The moment the statement becomes `false`, the while loop gets terminated and Ruby continues to execute the code after the loop.

For example, you want a program that will print the numbers 1 to10. Your code should look like this:

```
target_num = 0

while target_num < 10
      target_num = target_num + 1
      puts target_num
end
```

Let us explain the program line by line.

In the first line, the variable target_num has an initial value of 0.

The second line instructs the computer to keep executing the code within the `while` statement (the indented lines) as long as the variable target_num is less than 10.

In the third line, the variable target_num has a new value. The program adds 1 to its initial value 0. The variable target_num will have a new value each time it gets incremented by 1.

The fourth line instructs the computer to print or display the current value of target_num on the screen. It will continue to print the new value of target_num as long as target_num remains lower than or exactly 10. Keep in mind that the repetition only happens within the loop and it gets terminated once the goal of the while statement has been reached or the statement becomes false.

If you are thinking of ways to avoid using the while statement, you are in luck because there's another way to do it. However, after learning the long process you may want to switch back to while statement.

The long program looks like this:

```
# long_way.rb

target_num = 0
target_num = target_num + 1
puts target_num              #This will print 1

target_num = target_num + 1
puts target_num              #This will print 2

target_num = target_num + 1
puts target_num              #This will print 3

target_num = target_num + 1
puts target_num              #This will print 4

target_num = target_num + 1
puts target_num              #This will print 5

target_num = target_num + 1
puts target_num              #This will print 6

target_num = target_num + 1
puts target_num              #This will print 7

target_num = target_num + 1
puts target_num              #This will print 8

target_num = target_num + 1
puts target_num              #This will print 9

target_num = target_num + 1
puts target_num              #This will print 10
```

Is there any other way to print it? There is! Can you guess the other way to code the given program? Set your mind at work and try to find out before you look at the answer below. You can test yourself regarding your ability to code in Ruby at this stage.

If your hunch is correct, you can also do it this way:

```
puts 1
puts 2
puts 3
puts 4
puts 5
puts 6
puts 7
puts 8
puts 9
puts 10
```

The program with the while statement is still shorter than the two long programs.

What if the user prefers to input the number that he or she would like to print? You have no means of knowing the number that the user would type, unless you have psychic abilities. You cannot simply use either of the last given programs, and it is advisable to use the while statement for this particular case. Besides, even if you can guess the number that the user will choose, it would take you forever to code the program when the user type in 1,000,000.

Your code should look like this on the irb:

What if the user wants to print the numbers 1 to 10 in ascending order?

```
irb :001 > num = gets.chomp.to_i
10
=> 10
irb :002 > while num >= 0
irb :003 >    puts num
irb :004 >    num = num - 1
irb :005 > end
```

You can also write `num = num - 1` like this `num -= 1`. The output looks like this:

```
10
9
8
7
6
5
4
3
2
1
0
=> nil
```

When your program keeps on printing (somewhere in your code you must have triggered an infinite loop), always press `ctrl` and `c` to break the loop. If your program is not responding, it is possible that it was caught in an infinite loop.

Until Loop

Ruby programmers rarely use the `until` loop, which is the opposite of `while` loop. When using `until` loop, you need to reverse the process that takes place in the `while` loop.

In `while` loop, the computer will keep executing the code while the statement is true. In `until` loop, the computer will keep executing the code until the statement becomes true.

Take a look at this program:

```
# sample_until.rb

num1 = gets.chomp.to_i

until num1 < 0
  puts num1
  num1 -= 1
end
```

When the program asked the user for a number and he entered 5, the program will print '5' on the screen and decrement num1 by 1. When it enters the loop once more and found out that num1 is still not less than 0, it will again print num1 on screen. The number this time will be '4', which is the current value of num1. And again, num1 will decrement by 1 and will take on a new value.

When num1 turns 0, the code will still print it onscreen and decrement num1 by 1. At this point, num1 has become less than 0 (the current value of num1 by this time is -1), which prompts the `until` loop to stop the process since the statement has become true.

Try to write a program (similar to the sample program above) that will print a user input number in ascending order. Hint: use the `until` loop and make sure to reverse the operator.

Do/While loop

The `do/while` loop closely resembles the `while` loop. The conditional check in a `do/while` loop is placed at the loop's end as opposed to its usual place at the start of the loop.

Take a look at the program below that display a simple do/while loop. This program can give you a better understanding on how the loop works.

```
# execute_once_more.rb

loop do
  puts "Do it again? (Choose Yes or NO)"
  ans = gets.chomp
  if ans != "Yes"
    break
  end
end
```

The program prints the question and requires an input from the user. If it gets "Yes" for an answer, it will store the response to the variable named 'ans'. The program will keep asking the question while the answer remains "Yes". The loop gets terminated once the user typed in "No" or another answer for that matter. It only recognizes "Yes" as the only response that can get the loop going.

It can also be written like this:

```
# execute_once_more.rb (another version)

Begin
  puts "Do it again? (Choose Yes or NO)"
  ans = gets.chomp
end while ans == "Yes"
```

While the other version of the sample program for do/while loop works, it's not recommended by Ruby's creator.

For Loop

The for loop, in Ruby language, can be used to a collection of elements. The for loop has a definite end, unlike the while loop where it could encounter a problem. In while loop, there is always a risk of causing an infinite loop if you are not careful in writing your code or program.

This is the correct syntax to write the for loop:

```
for z in 1 .. x do
```

It begins with the reserved word `for` followed by a variable name, in this case z, after that comes the reserved word `in` followed by the range or list of elements to loop over.

If you need to loop over a collection of elements in a range or array, then the best choice is `for` loop. In Ruby, there is a special type called `range` that captures a collection of elements. For example 1..4 is a range that captures the integers 1, 2, 3, and 4. After execution, the `for` loop also returns a collection of elements.

```
# sample_program_for.rb

for z in 1..10 do
    puts z
end
```

This program will yield this result:

```
1
2
3
4
5
6
7
8
9
10
=> 1..10
```

What if you were asked to write the same program in which the user will provide the input the extent of the range?

Treat this as a programming exercise for you to work on. Try to answer this on your own and you will know the answer near the end of this subchapter.

You can also use array, something like this:

```
# sample_program_for.rb
```

```
b = [1, 2, 3, 4, 5, 6, 7, 8, 9, 10]

for a in b do
  puts a
end
```

Here are two more samples using array:

```
# sample_program2_for.rb

b = [123, 456, 789, 111, 222]

for a in b do
  puts a
end

# sample_program3_for.rb

b = ["Chelsea", "Ana", "Charlie", "Maxi", "Gabbey"]

for a in b do
  puts a
end
```

The for loop passes through all the values contained in the array and prints each one on the computer screen. The loop automatically stops when the last element in the array is printed.

Before we discuss another sample program, here is the answer to the programming exercise that you were asked to do:

There are a lot of ways to loop and you need to decide which one is the best for your available data.

CONDITIONALS, ITERATORS, AND RECURSION

Conditionals within Loops

Next and Break in the Conditional Loop

Iterators

Recursion

Conditionals within Loops

We want to create precise and effective loops. We can actually incorporate conditional flow control within the loops to modify their behavior. For our opening salvo for this subchapter, let us use the `if` statement in a `while` loop. In this sample program we will introduce you to `.odd?` method (this and other Ruby methods can be found in Ruby documentation).

```ruby
# while_with_conditional.rb

z = 0

while z <= 20
  if z.odd?
    puts z
  end
  z += 1
end
```

In the sample program, variable `z` is assigned the value 0 (initialization). The `while` statement says that the process it contains must be executed while variable `z` is less than or equal to 0. However, there is a conditional `if` statement within the `while` loop. It demands that only odd numbers from 1 to 20 must be printed.

The variable `z` gets incremented by 1. When it loops over, the new value of `z` is 1, which is still less than 20. The loop will only stop when the variable `z` is higher than 20.

Try the same program using `.even?` method instead of `.odd?` and see what happens.

Next and Break in the Conditional Loop

The reserved words `break` and `next` can be used in the conditional loop as well. When `next` is used in a loop, it will jump from the line where `next` is located to the subsequent loop iteration. The code beneath it will not be executed.

```
# next_conditional_loop.rb

digit = 0

while digit <= 20
  if digit == 5
    digit += 1
    next
  elsif digit.odd?
    puts digit
  end
  digit += 1
end
```

You will get this output:

```
1
3
7
9
11
13
15
17
19
=> nil
```

The presence of `next` has prevented number 5 from being printed.

When break is used in a loop, it will prompt the computer to quickly terminate the loop and prevent the execution of other code within the loop.

```ruby
# break_conditional_loop.rb

unit = 0

while unit <= 20
  if unit == 11
    break
  elsif unit.odd?
    puts unit
  end
  unit += 1
end
```

You will get this output:

```
1
3
5
7
9
=> nil
```

As you can see, the number 11 is not printed as well as the rest of number within the range due to the presence of break. It automatically stopped the computer from executing the rest of the code or from looping.

Iterators

When you want methods that let you operate on each item in a collection and can naturally loop over a given set of data, then it is best to use iterators.

You already know that an array has ordered list. What if you want to print the names listed in the array on the screen without returning a nil? You can use the method named each.

```ruby
# perform_method_each.rb
```

```
aka = ['Chels', 'Ana', 'Chai', 'Max', 'Gab',
'Allan', 'Ruth']

aka.each { |aka| puts aka }
```

The `.each` method loops through each item in the array starting from the very first element, which is 'Chels'. It executes the code within the block (from the first curly brace to the last curly brace). Keep in mind that the starting and ending points of a block are determined by the curly braces ({ }).

Let us take a look at another sample program:

```
# sample_each.rb

aka = ['Chels', 'Ana', 'Chai', 'Max', 'Gab',
'Allan', 'Ruth']
count = 1

aka.each do |aka|
  puts "#{count}. #{aka}"
  count += 1
end
```

This is the output:

```
1. Chels
2. Ana
3. Chai
4. Max
5. Gab
6. Allan
7. Ruth
=> ["Chels", "Ana", "Chai", "Max", "Gab", "Allan",
"Ruth"]
```

The variable `count` was added to serve as a counter for each name to create a numbered list output.

There are several `iterator` methods in Ruby, and you will get to use a number of them in a long run as you develop your programming skills. Most Ruby programmers prefer to use iterators when they need something to loop over a group of elements.

Like most Ruby programmers, you may find iterators more to your liking or you may also find other methods more acceptable than the others. It's really a matter of preference and it is best if you have a number of choices to choose from than be content with just one or two options.

Recursion

Ruby offers another way to create a loop called recursion. It gives the ability of calling a method within itself. To make it easier to understand, let us create a program.

Here's the scenario: you were tasked to create a program that must double the amount of a given number and to continue doubling the amount of each answer you obtain. For the said program, it is best to create a method like this:

```
def double(num)
  puts num * 2
end
```

Then you can do this on your irb:

```
irb(main):001:0> def double(num)
irb(main):002:1>    puts num * 2
irb(main):003:1> end
=> :double
irb(main):004:0> double (2)
4
=> nil
irb(main):005:0> double (4)
8
=> nil
irb(main):006:0> double (8)
16
=> nil
irb(main):006:0> double (16)
```

104

```
32
=> nil
irb(main):006:0> double (32)
64
=> nil
```

You can simplify the program using `recursion`. We will use the same double method. You can do it this way:

```
irb(main):001:0> def double(num)
irb(main):002:1>   puts num
irb(main):003:1>   if num < 60
irb(main):004:2>     double(num * 2)
irb(main):005:2>   end
irb(main):006:1> end
=> :double
irb(main):007:0> double(2)
2
4
8
16
32
64
=> nil
```

CHAPTER 8: MORE ON ARRAYS AND HASHES

ARRAYS

Modifying Arrays

Array Iteration

Nested Arrays

Evaluating Arrays

Modifying Arrays

In the previous chapter, you already have an idea regarding arrays and hashes. In this chapter, we will try to know more about these two.

Let's say you have this kind of array named x:

```
irb :001 > X = [7, 'Al', 14.3, 'Claire']
```

You need to assign the array to a variable so you can do anything with it. As you can see, array x contains different types of data.

If you want to print the first element of array x on screen you can do this:

```
irb :002 > puts x.first
7
=> nil
```

What if you want to print the next one in the list? Go back to the chapter that discussed the array index if you forgot.

```
irb :003 > puts x[1]
Al
=> nil
```

If you would like to print the last element you can do this:

```
irb :004 > puts x.last
Claire
=> nil
```

If you need to print the other elements in the array, use an index. It is really important to practice what you have learned so that you won't forget.

Modifying Arrays

What if you want to remove an element from a particular array? There are several methods that you can use and some of them will be discussed in the succeeding sections.

You can use .pop when you want remove the last item of the array. If you can recall, we already discussed a bit about .pop earlier.

```
irb :005 > x.pop
=> "Claire"
```

To verify if the last element was removed:

```
irb :006 > x
=> [7, 'Al', 14.3]
```

You can use .push when you want to add an item to the array.

```
irb :007 > x.push('Claire')
=> [7, 'Al', 14.3, 'Claire']
```

Another way to add an item to the array is to use the shovel operator <<. Take note that the deleted or added item to the array is permanently deleted or added.

Let us add another item to the array.

```
irb :008 > x << 'Hello'
=> [7, 'Al', 14.3, 'Claire', 'Hello']
```

Now, let's talk about map method. This method returns a new array when it iterates over it. Another method that does the same is called collect.

```
irb :001 > this = [1, 2, 3, 4,5]
=> [1, 2, 3, 4,5]
irb :002 > this.map { |x| x * 2 }
=> [2, 4, 6, 8, 10]
irb :003 > this.collect { |x| x * 2 }
=> [2, 4, 6, 8, 10]
irb :004 > this
=> [1, 2, 3, 4, 5]
```

After applying the map or collect method, the original array remains the same. The applied methods do not alter the caller.

There is also a delete method that you can use if you want to permanently remove a certain item in the array by accessing the index. Keep in mind that when this method called, it means you would like to change your array. If there is a particular segment in your program that also uses the array, it will get affected.

```
irb :005 > this.delete_at(2)
=> 3
irb :006 > this
=> [1, 2, 4, 5]
```

What if you don't know the index of the element or entity that you wish to delete? You can still use the method delete because it can trace and remove the occurrence of the element's existence in the array.

```
irb :001 > pets = ["fish", "iguana", "dog", "fish", "rabbit"]
=> ["fish", "iguana", "dog", "fish", "rabbit"]
irb :002 > pets.delete("fish")
=> "fish"
irb :003 > pets
=> ["iguana", "dog", "rabbit"]
```

The initial array listed 2 instances of 'fish'. When delete method was applied, all the instances of 'fish' were removed. If you want to add just one, you can use the shovel operator or push.

Array Iteration

In the chapter where we discussed about loops, you learned about each, which you can use if you want to perform iteration on your array. Ruby has a number of similar methods. Let us discuss select.

This method allows iteration on an array and yields a new array that contains the items that yield true to the provided expression.

```
irb :001 > num = [1, 2, 3, 4, 5]
 => [1, 2, 3, 4, 5]
irb :002 > num.select { |num| num < 3 }
 => [1, 2]
irb :003 > num
 => [1, 2, 3, 4, 5]
```

In the sample program, the purpose of the select method is to select all the numbers that are less than 3 and be able to return the selected numbers in an array. However, it does not change the initial array (no mutation).

Nested Arrays

Nested arrays are actually arrays that contain arrays. If you would like to keep a list of the participants in each team, you can make this kind of array:

```
irb :001 > set = [['Joelle', 'Vicki'], ['Anne',
'Blake'], ['Al', 'Ene']]
=> [["Joelle", "Vicki"], ["Anne", "Blake"], ["Al",
"Ene"]]
```

You can use an index to access each team.

```
irb :002 > set [0]
=> ["Joelle", "Vicki"]
```

Evaluating Arrays

When you need to compare the equality of arrays, you use ==.

```
irb :001 > x = [1, 2, 3,4]
=> [1, 2, 3, 4]
irb :002 > y = [2, 3, 4, 5]
=> [2, 3, 4, 5]
irb :003 > x == y
=> false
irb :004 > y.pop # this will yield [2,3,4]
=> 5
irb :005 > y.unshift(1) # this will yield[1,2,3,4]
=> [1, 2, 3]
irb :006 > x == y
=> true
```

As you can see, the first time that the program tested the equality between the arrays it returned a `false` value. We need to make it `true`. We need to use the `pop` and `unshift` method on array y.

You already know what `pop` does, how about `unshift`? Just think of it as the exact opposite of `pop`.

ARRAY METHODS AND HASHES

Typical Array Methods

The Methods Named Each and Map

Hashes

Iterating over Hashes

Typical Array Methods

There are so many array methods and this subchapter intends to give you an introduction to some of them. You may want to keep this link handy: <u>Array class</u>.

1. `include?`

The method `include?` checks whether the array contains a certain argument. This method returns true or false. It is something like this:

```
irb: 001 > z = [1, 2, 3]
=> [1, 2, 3]
irb: 002 > z.include?(4)
=> false
irb: 003 > z.include?(2)
=> true
```

2. `flatten`

As the name implies, `flatten` has the ability to turn a nested or two-dimensional array into one-dimensional. It literally flattens the array.

```
irb: 001 > x = [1, [2, 3], 4, [5, 6, 7]]
=> [1, [2, 3], 4, [5, 6, 7]]
irb: 002 > x.flatten
=> [1, 2, 3, 4, 5, 6, 7]
```

111

When you want to check if the content of the array has changed, simply type the name of the array and hit enter. The above program will give you this:

```
irb: 003 > x
=> [1, [2, 3], 4, [5, 6, 7]]
```

As you can see, the array still holds it original content. You can do the same test to all the arrays that you use.

3. sort

The method sort is helpful when you want a sorted array.

```
irb :001 > z = [4, 2, 8, 5, 3, 1, 7]
=> [5, 3, 8, 2, 4, 1]
irb :002 > z.sort
=> [1, 2, 3, 4, 5, 7, 8]
```

4. product

The method product has the ability to combine arrays. It returns the combination of elements from both arrays.

```
irb :001 > [4, 5, 6].product([7, 9])
=> [[4, 7], [4, 9], [5, 7], [5, 9], [6, 7], [6, 9]]
```

These are just some of the methods that you can use on your array.

The Methods Named Each and Map

The method each is usually used in for loop and it offers a simple way of performing iteration on the elements in the array. Take a look at the sample below:

```
samp = [1, 2, 3]
samp.each { |any_variable| puts any_variable }
1
2
3
=> [1, 2, 3]
```

The sample above is the most typical way of using each. You can also modify the items in the array and still returns the original array. Take note that you can use any variable name, but you need to be consistent in using the same variable name all throughout the program for that particular array.

```
samp = [1, 2, 3]
samp.each { |any_variable| puts any_variable + 3 }
4
5
6
=> [1, 2, 3]
```

The method map is similar with each, except it returns the value that map has created. However, the original content of the array still remains the same.

```
another = [1, 2, 3]
another.map { |y| y*2 }
=> [2, 4, 6]
```

What if you use puts?

```
another = [1, 2, 3]
another.map { |y| puts y*2 }
=> [nil, nil, nil]
```

You already know that puts returns nil. Each time the program calls upon the block, it returns nil.

The methods map and each are important but because they resemble each other so much, learning them can be a tad confusing. Remember this: for iteration you need to use each, for transformation you need to use map.

Hashes

Array has index and hash has keys. You already learned in the previous chapter that hash entries are key-value pairs within the curly braces. Take a look at these samples:

```
irb :001 > fresh_hash = {name: 'Betty'}
```

113

```
=> {:name=>'Betty'}
```

```
# sample 2
```

```
irb :002 > bio = { height: '5 ft', weight: '110 lbs'
}
=> {:height=>'5 ft', :weight=>'110 lbs'}
```

What if you want to add some more?

```
irb :003 > bio [:hair] = 'blonde'
=> "blonde"
irb :004 > bio
=> {:height=>'5 ft', :weight=>'110 lbs',
:hair=>'brown'}
irb :005> bio [:age] = 22
=> 22
irb :006> bio
=> {:height=>'5 ft', :weight=>'110 lbs',
:hair=>'blonde', :age=>22}
```

You can also remove an entry from the current hash.

```
irb :007 > bio.delete(:weight)
=> "110 lbs"
irb :008 > bio
=> {:height=>'5 ft', :hair=>'blonde', :age=>22}
```

Do you want to retrieve the information from the hash? Simply do this:

```
irb :009 > bio [:hair]
=> "blonde"
```

You can also merge two hashes together. You can use either of these two:

```
# choice 1
```

```
irb :010 > bio.merge (fresh_hash)
=> {:height=>'5 ft', :hair=>'blonde', :age=>22,
:name=>'Betty'}
irb :011 > bio.merge
=> {:height=>"5 ft", :hair=>"blonde", :age=>22}
```

```
# choice 2
```

```
irb :010 > bio.merge!(fresh_hash)
```

```
=> {:height=>'5 ft', :hair=>'blonde', :age=>22,
:name=>'Betty'}
irb :011 > bio.merge!(fresh_hash)
=> {:height=>"5 ft", :hair=>"blonde", :age=>22,
:name=>"Betty"}
```

Notice that in 'choice 1' `.merge` was used and the two arrays successfully merged. When you check the current content of array bio, you will see that there's no change. In 'choice 2' `.merge` was used with a bang operator (!). When you check the current content of array bio, you will see that it has been completely modified.

Iterating over Hashes

Iterating over hashes is comparable to iterating over arrays, only with slight differences. We will use method `each` to demonstrate. However, for this program we are going to assign a variable for the key as well as the value. We will use variable 'ref' for the key and variable 'content' for the value.

You can try to create your own program using the same pattern and experiment if you want.

```
# iterate_hashes.rb

record = {name: 'Clark', height: '6 ft', weight:
'140 lbs', hair: 'black', status: 'single'}

record.each do |ref, content|
  puts "Bob's #{ref} is #{content}"
end
```

When you try this on irb, you will see this:

MORE ON HASHES

Hashes vs. Arrays

Hash Keys

Commonly Used Hash Methods

Hashes vs. Arrays

When is the best time to use hashes or arrays? You can actually use an array or a hash in your program. There are no rules that might restrict you from choosing one over the other. However, you may want to ask these questions in order to choose the best one to access or manipulate the data for the program that you intend to write.

1. Do you need a queue or a stack structure?

Arrays are your best choice if you want last-in-first-out stacks or first-in-first-out queues.

2. Does the data need to be linked to a specific tag?

If your answer is yes, then it is wise to use a hash. If you are working with data that have no specific label, you can use array.

3. Do you want to follow a certain order?

Although hashes also maintain order, it is wise to use array. Most programmers that would like to gain access to an ordered list of elements prefer arrays.

As you develop your familiarity with the two data structures, you will be able to tell in one glance which one to choose for a particular program. You need to keep experimenting and working with both data structures to find out which will work best in a given situation.

Hash Keys

So far, we've been using symbols as keys in all the sample programs that used hashes. Aside from the symbols, you can also use integer, array, string, float, and hash as keys.

```
# hash as key

irb :001 > {{var_key: "key"} => "hash here is used
as a key"}
=> {{:var_key=>"key"}=>"hash as a key"}

# float as key

irb :002 > {86. 895 => "using float"}
=> {45.324=>"using float"}

# integer as key

irb :003 > {7 => "seven"}
=> {7=>"seven"}

# array as key

irb :004 > {["age"] => "28"}
=> {["age"]=>"28"}

# string as key

irb :005 > {"color" => "cyan blue"}
=> {"color"=>"cyan blue"}
```

As you can see, hashes offer diversity and you can store almost everything that you want. Also, you need to use this style => for the key-value pairing (as you can see from the samples above).

Commonly Used Hash Methods

Like arrays, hashes have so many methods. We advice to keep this link handy: Hash class. We will discuss some of the commonly used hash methods.

1. has_key?

This method checks whether a hash contains a specific key. It returns `true` or `false` value.

```
irb :001 > name_plus_hair = { "BJ" => "blonde",
"Clark" => "black", "Al" => "brown"}
=> {"BJ"=>"blonde", "Clark"=>"black", "Al"=>"brown"}
irb :002 > name_plus_hair.has_key?("Joe")
=> false
irb :003 > name_plus_hair.has_key?("Al")
=> true
```

2. select

This method returns any key-value pairs when you pass a block. The pair should evaluate to `true` when ran through the block.

```
irb :004 > name_plus_hair.select { |kee,val| kee ==
"BJ" }
=> {"BJ"=>"blonde"}
irb :005 > name_plus_hair.select { |kee,val| (kee ==
"BJ") || (val == "brown") }
=> {"BJ"=>"blonde", "Al"=>"brown"}
```

3. fetch

When you use this method in your program, it returns or fetches the value of the key if there is such key in your hash. You can also include an option to still return an answer if the key is not included in the hash. Ruby usually returns an error message in the absence of the key being searched.

```
irb :006 > name_plus_hair.fetch("Clark")
=> "black"
irb :007 > name_plus_hair.fetch ("Joe")
=> KeyError: key not found: "Joe"


irb :008 > name_plus_hair.fetch ("Joe", "Joe is not
included")
=> "Joe is not included"
```

4. to_a

This method returns the hash in array version when you use it. This method does not permanently modify the hash.

```
irb :009 > name_plus_hair.to_a
=> [["BJ", "blonde"], ["Clark", "black"], ["Al",
"brown"]]
irb :010 > name_plus_hair
=> { "BJ" => "blonde", "Clark" => "black", "Al" =>
"brown"}
```

When you check the content of the hash, nothing has changed.

5. `keys` and `values`

You use the `keys` and `values` methods when you want to retrieve all the values or all the keys of your hash. Notice that the returned values or keys are in array.

```
irb :0011 > name_plus_hair.keys
=> ["BJ", "Clark", "Al"]
irb :0012 > name_plus_hair.values
=> ["blonde", "black", "brown"]
```

You can go back to the previous exercises and practice them. You can also make some modifications or try a different approach for each program that you have done. Remember that there is more than one way to tackle the problem.

Continue practicing your programming skills and try to reach the advanced level.

CONCLUSION:

The Ruby language is not difficult to learn, but you need to have ample amount of patience in memorizing the Ruby documentation. It helps a lot in creating a readable and efficient program. Remember that everything that you have learned from this book is just the beginning. You must continue to hone your Ruby programming skill and be an expert Ruby programmer.

Practice makes perfect and it is advisable to allot time to do some Ruby programming exercises. Read advanced Ruby programming materials and you may even gain an opportunity to choose a more productive path.

OTHER BOOKS BY iCODE ACADEMY

If you want to know more about other books from the series, click on the link in each title:

Book 1 : Python For Beginners: Your Guide To Easily Learn Python Programming in 7 Days

Book 2 : <u>Programming For Beginners: 3 Manuscripts in 1 Bundle - Python For Beginners, Java Programming and Html & CSS For Beginners</u>

Book 3: **<u>HTML & CSS For Beginners: Your Step by Step Guide to Easily HtmL & Css Programming in 7 Days</u>**

Book 4: <u>C Programming for Beginners: Your Guide to Easily Learn C Programming In 7 Days</u>

Book 5: JQuery For Beginners: Your Guide To Easily Learn Jquery Programming in 7 Days

Book 6: HTML5 and CSS3 for Beginners: Your Guide To Easily Learn Html5 and Css3 in 7 Days

Book 7: Ruby For Beginners: Your Guide To Easily Learn Html5 and Css3 in 7 Days

DID YOU ENJOY THIS BOOK?

I want to thank you for purchasing and reading this book. I really hope you got a lot out of it.

Can I ask a quick favor though?

If you enjoyed this book I would really appreciate it if you could leave me a positive review on Amazon.

I love getting feedback from my customers and reviews on Amazon really do make a difference. I read all my reviews and would really appreciate your thoughts.

Thanks so much.

iCode Academy

p.s. You can click here to go directly to the book on Amazon and leave your review.